TOM
University College London (UCL) and visiting professor at New
York University. He is the author of six books and writes regular
blogs for Harvard Business Review and Psychology Today. He lives
in London and New York, and frequently appears in the media. You
can learn more about Tomas Chamorro-Premuzic on his website
http://www.drtomascp.co

70001643796 2

CONFIDENCE

Overcoming
Low Self-Esteem,
Insecurity,
and Self-Doubt

Tomas Chamorro-Premuzic, PhD

P
PROFILE BOOKS

First published in Great Britain in 2013 by
PROFILE BOOKS LTD
3A Exmouth House
Pine Street
London EC1R 0JH
www.profilebooks.com

First published in the United States of America in 2013 by
Hudson Street Press, a member of the Penguin Group (USA)

10 9 8 7 6 5 4 3 2 1

Printed and bound in Great Britain by
Clays, Bungay, Suffolk

A CIP catalogue record for this book is available from the British Library.

ISBN 978 1 78125 196 6
eISBN 978 1 78283 017 7

The paper this book is printed on is certified by the © 1996 Forest Stewardship Council A.C.
(FSC). It is ancient-forest friendly. The printer holds FSC chain of custody SGS-COC-2061

to Zdenka Premuzic
(who does not need to read this book)

Contents

Dear Reader:

If you picked up this book to increase your confidence, you are not alone. Millions of people have low confidence and most of them worry about it, not least because it is hard to boost our confidence at will. The good news is that low confidence is less problematic than you think. In fact, although society places a great deal of importance on being confident, there are no genuine benefits except feeling good. In fact, lower confidence is key to gaining competence, which is the only effective strategy for gaining genuine confidence—confidence that is warranted by one's actual competence.

Confidence is feeling able and competence is being able, but how are the two related? Too many people ignore this question and simply assume that higher confidence is advantageous per se. Although this assumption is unfounded, it has nonetheless encouraged a mindless and often self-destructive quest for higher confidence. Indeed, in much of the Western world, particularly the United States, the assumption is that more confidence is always better.[1] If it weren't for this assumption, you might not even be reading this book. There is no reason to be ashamed of our low confidence.

The main difference between people who lack confidence and those who don't is that the former are unable (or unwilling) to distort reality in their favor. That's right, the successful distortion of reality is the chief underlying reason so many people don't experience low confidence when they should.

Whereas pessimism leads to realism, optimism promotes the fabrication of alternative realities—lying, not to others, but to ourselves. There is no reason to envy people who appear confident, even if they are also successful; their success is usually the cause rather than consequence of their high confidence. The idea that we must do something about our low confidence is by and large the result of popular myths, which are not hard to debunk.

If you are concerned about your low confidence, this book will teach you what you can do about it. The main lesson is that you should aspire not to have high confidence, but to have high competence, and I will show you how to make that happen. Confidence will follow more easily when you can back it up with real accomplishments (and even then, it may be better to remain relatively unassertive).

Approach this book with as critical and open a mind as you can. Do not assume that the power to become instantly more confident is simply in your hands *or* that high confidence should be your goal. Moreover, don't assume that having low confidence will harm your chances of doing well in life. Or if you prefer to make these assumptions, be ready to have them challenged.

Tomas Chamorro-Premuzic, PhD

February 2013

CONFIDENCE

1

Confidence Ain't Competence

It is a cliché that most clichés are true, but then like most clichés, that cliché is untrue.   —Stephen Fry

The Difference Between Feeling and Being Able

Biographers are quick to attribute the success of eminent people to their colossal levels of confidence, while downplaying the roles of talent and hard work, as if it were in anyone's hands (or minds) to achieve exceptional levels of success merely through sheer self-belief. In line, magazines and popular blogs grossly exaggerate the role of confidence in determining fame and success. Consider the following examples:[1]

"No matter what you do, be sure to love yourself for doing it."
"If you have confidence you will reach any goal you have; but without it, you have no chance of being successful."
"If you love yourself, your life will be perfect."
"We all admire confident people—confidence is the most important asset in life and it will always lead to success and happiness."

"We can all teach ourselves to be confident and then all
   our problems will be solved."
"Confident people are ten times more successful than
   those who lack confidence."

There are three big problems with these types of claims. First,
it is not easy to make your confidence soar, just like that. If it were,
nobody would worry about low confidence; we would just extinguish
it like we do thirst or hunger. Second, even if we succeeded at deliberately boosting our confidence, it would not bring us any genuine
success. Contrary to what some biographers and self-nominated experts suggest, Barack Obama did not become the first black president in U.S. history because he was confident; Sir Richard Branson,
the founder of Virgin, did not establish four hundred companies
because of his confidence; Madonna has not sold three hundred
million records because of her self-belief; and Michael Jordan, Mu-
hammad Ali, and Roger Federer did not achieve total domination of
their sports because they felt good about themselves. The reason
these exceptional achievers have confidence is that they are exceptionally competent. It takes an extraordinary amount of talent—and
even more hard work—to attain such levels of competence. In fact,
the only unusual thing about these people's confidence is that it is
an accurate reflection of their competence. This sets them apart
from the majority of superconfident people, who are just not very
competent.

The third problem is arguably the most serious one. The illusion
that high confidence can help us achieve anything we want puts an
incredible amount of pressure on us to feel assertive, and to translate that assertiveness into success. As a consequence, those who lack
confidence feel guilty and ashamed, and those who feel confident

have unrealistic expectations about what their confidence will help them accomplish. The high confidence *premium* is such that people are prepared to do just about anything to attain and maintain extreme positive self-views, equating feeling great with being great. The result is a society that mistakes self-importance for importance and self-admiration for admiration, driving more and more people to be obsessed only with themselves.

Me, Me, Me (the Narcissistic Society)

Narcissism—think Donald Trump or Paris Hilton—is a state of mind characterized by unrealistic feelings of grandiosity and inflated self-confidence. Narcissists are self-centered and feel superior to everyone else; they pay no attention to negative comments from others and dismiss negative feedback. Narcissists are also manipulative and don't mind exploiting people in order to attain power, fame, or success.[2] The word derives from the Greek myth of Narcissus, a beautiful hunter who was so self-obsessed that he paid no attention to others. In order to punish him, the goddess Nemesis attracted Narcissus to a pond, where he fell in love with his own reflection, not realizing that he was looking at himself. One version of the story says Narcissus drowned trying to kiss his own image; another version, that he remained on his own by the pond until his death, infatuated with his own reflection and unable to relate to anyone else.

There are many reasons to suggest that we are living in a narcissistic era. Indeed, the fact that you may worry about your low levels of confidence is by and large the result of living in a world obsessed with maintaining inflated self-views and high levels of confidence.

In the United States, narcissism levels have been rising for decades. Psychologist Jean Twenge[3] has been tracking national increases of narcissism for years. In one of her studies, Dr. Twenge analyzed data from more than 40,000 students from hundreds of U.S. colleges. In the 1950s, only 12 percent of students described themselves as "an important person"; by the 1980s, the figure had increased to 80 percent. Her data also revealed that between 1982 and 2006 alone, the number of narcissistic students rose from 15 percent to 25 percent, with an even bigger increase found among the women—surprising, since women are typically less narcissistic than men.

Levels of self-esteem—the most generic measure of confidence—have been rising exponentially in the past decades: In 2006, 80 percent of U.S. school students reported self-esteem levels that were higher than the average for 1988.[4] Even more worryingly, a large-scale study by the National Institutes of Health, the main U.S. government agency for funding biomedical and health research, reported that 10 percent of Americans in their twenties met the criteria for clinical (severe) narcissism, compared to just 3 percent of people in their sixties.[5]

It is hard to put these increases into perspective. There are no comparable generational rises for any other psychological trait—aggression, greed, anxiety, IQ, you name it. Unless you are talking thousands of years, people tend not to change much over time. The one increase comparable to the rise in narcissism levels (during a similar time period) is the rise in obesity levels, which increased more than 200 percent from 1950 to 2010.[6] Unlike narcissism gains, however, obesity gains are an acknowledged epidemic. Self-esteem is an unobservable feeling, which makes narcissism rises less apparent than obesity rises.

It would be good if narcissism gains reflected increases in

well-being. However, all they indicate is that a growing number of people are obsessed with maintaining extreme positive self-views and unrealistically high levels of confidence. This obsession explains the near-universality of the celebrity cult, with a substantial proportion of the population worshipping those who worship themselves. Indeed, millions of people around the world now aspire to be like Paris Hilton, Simon Cowell, or Lady Gaga, who has more followers on Twitter than anyone else. The explosion of social media sites also allows us all to experience glimpses of stardom firsthand: You don't have to be Lady Gaga to tweet about what you had for breakfast or tell your followers that your cat is sick, that you had a good workout, or that you are checking in at Starbucks; the only difference is that you are not Lady Gaga.

Unsurprisingly, there are now one billion people on Facebook. Consider the case of a college student who has six hundred friends on Facebook and is constantly updating his status. This student will spend much of his time monitoring other people's Facebook usage in hopes that they will "like" his activity and write positive comments on his wall (on average, students check their Facebook account at least ten times per day). He will also engage in inappropriate self-disclosure and post thousands of intimate photographs. Happy times? Not really. In fact, research has shown that people who spend a great deal of time on Facebook have lower levels of academic performance and are typically unhappier, especially when they perceive that their friends (who are uploading their own pictures onto Facebook) are happier than they are.[7]

In our narcissistic society, Facebook enables users to create both a confidence and competence *illusion*, portraying themselves as successful and confident, without, however, persuading themselves—and at best others—that they are either. Facebook is particularly appealing to narcissists because it enables them to compensate for their lack of genuine friends by collecting a large number of virtual "friends" who can play the role of fans. Reassuringly for narcissists, Facebook does not allow users to dislike other users' activity—we are only allowed to "like" what others do.[8] Unsurprisingly, a recent study found that Facebook users tend to be more narcissistic and exhibitionistic than nonusers, leading the authors to conclude that "Facebook specifically gratifies the narcissistic individual's need to engage in self-promoting and superficial behaviour."[9]

A culture of narcissism makes inflated self-views the norm, but if we all paid attention just to ourselves and lacked interest in anyone else, then we'd be condemned to a selfish and isolated life. It would be good if people's delusions of grandiosity actually enticed them to work hard to attain any kind of grandeur. However, these delusions have precisely the reverse effect, not least because they are close to unattainable. Indeed, the more narcissistic people are, the more unrealistic their expectations will tend to be; and the more unrealistic your expectations are, the more likely you are to end up being depressed when you finally come to terms with the fact that you cannot achieve them. In line, rates of depression have been soaring steadily in the past decades. For instance, from the early 1990s to the early 2000s, rates of depression in the United States increased from 3 percent to 7 percent, a figure that has since doubled.[10] As a matter of fact, depression is now considered one of the leading causes of disability in the world, with current estimates indicating that more than 120 million people worldwide suffer from it.[11] In the United States, depression affects at least one in ten males and two in ten females.[12]

Wanting Versus Needing Confidence (and Coke)

Have you ever craved an ice-cold bottle of Coke? We all have—and yet, there is no real need or biological justification for it. Likewise, millions of people in the world crave high confidence without realizing that they don't really need it. However, whereas even the most fanatical Coke consumers realize the drink is unhealthy (at least in its regular and sugary version), few people understand that there are no genuine advantages to feeling good about yourself. Instead, most people seem to believe that if they feel good about themselves and have confidence, they will accomplish anything they want, and that if they don't, they will never manage to excel at anything. The result is a society in which people want confidence more than they need it: a feel-good culture in which the quest for confidence has eclipsed any interest in competence, and most people mistake feeling well for doing well.

The Coke comparison works on many levels. There are few stronger demonstrations of the appeal of our feel-good culture than Coca-Cola, one of the most successful brands of our time. Why does Coke have more Facebook fans than anyone or anything else?[13] Is it because they sell black fizzy syrup? Not really. Just like the caffeine and sugar in Coke make you feel good—a quick and unhealthy fix, made marginally healthier if you consume Diet Coke— Coke's brand empowers consumers to feel secure by endorsing a spoiled lifestyle in which the main fixation is short-term hedonism. Take a look at some of Coke's slogans over the years:[14]

- 1963: "Things go better with Coke."
- 1979: "Have a Coke and a smile."
- 1989: "Can't beat the feeling."

In 2010, Coca-Cola released a YouTube video ("The Happiness Machine") of a Coke vending machine placed in a college. The video was filmed with hidden cameras and featured the reactions of students to the freebies—flowers, sandwiches, and, of course, Coke—provided by the machine. The clip, which rapidly exceeded three million YouTube hits, shows how feeling good is still a central part of Coke's DNA. A year later—and after some thirty variations of the original Happiness Machine clip—Coke released another video ("The Happiness Truck"), made in Rio de Janeiro, Brazil. This time, the vending machine was an actual truck dispensing yet more happiness products: soccer balls, beach gear, and even a surfboard . . . plus, of course, Coke.

Despite the fact that Coke is now known to be unhealthy, people around the world continue to consume larger quantities of it than ever before. This increase in consumption mirrors the increase in demand for many other feel-good products. For example, the past five decades have seen TV viewing figures soar. In the United States, the average household has a TV set switched on for seven hours a day.[15] The amount of time spent watching TV in the United States (a combined 250 billion hours per year) is equivalent to a potential economic growth of 1.25 trillion dollars, based merely on minimum wage salaries paid for that time. Meanwhile, the average American teenager spends nine hundred hours per year in school, versus fifteen hundred watching TV. Yet most Americans don't think they watch too much TV.

The past few decades have also been marked by exponential growth in the self-help market, which includes books, CDs, seminars, and workshops designed to help people boost their confidence. Between 2005 and 2008 (the year of the most recent economic collapse), demand for self-help products grew by almost 14 percent,[16] and there has been further growth since then, with the self-help industry worth around eleven billion dollars now.[17] The vast majority of these products are based on the premise that boosting our confidence will solve all our problems, but there is little evidence for the beneficial effects of self-help products. In 2005, journalist Steve Salerno published a well-researched critique of the whole feel-good market (titled *SHAM: How the Self-help Movement Made America Helpless*), reporting that 80 percent of self-help consumers are "serial customers," who purchase and use a great many products.[18] This is consistent with Dr. Twenge's finding that rates of depression have increased with narcissism and self-worth levels over the past decades.

Like Coke, then, self-help books create an addictive demand for a quick feel-good fix. And as with Coke, there are noxious long-term effects of being too obsessed with one's own feelings. Unfortunately, repeated exposure to the message that we must feel good at any cost sets unrealistically high expectations for both our confidence and our competence: The more we are told that the norm is to feel good, the worse we feel when we don't achieve it; the more we persuade ourselves that confidence brings competence, the more disappointed we are when the attained confidence does not bring us competence—unless we become delusional in order to avoid feeling disappointment. The result is a vicious circle: Our feel-good obsession causes unhappiness, which perpetuates the demand for self-help books and other feel-good products, which foment our feel-good obsession.

Just as there is a difference between competence and confidence, then, there is a difference between feeling and being good. When it comes to competence, feeling good does not increase the probability of being good. Moreover, although you may want confidence, it is not really what you need—what you need is competence rather than confidence. Admittedly, boosting our confidence levels would be a worthy enterprise if it helped us be more successful or if it increased our actual competence. However, there is no real evidence that high confidence causes competence.

Higher Confidence Does Not Cause Competence

We've already begun to explore and debunk common misconceptions about the relationship between confidence and competence. Now let's take a look at the numbers. The relationship between competence and confidence is very weak. To be more precise, the average correlation between confidence and competence is around .30.[19] What does this mean? Imagine you meet someone who is confident, and you want to guess whether that person is competent or not. If instead of relying on the default 50 percent chance rate (yes/no) you take into account the scientific evidence on the relationship between confidence and competence, you would have a 65 percent probability of guessing whether the person is competent or not.[20]

No matter how large a correlation is, it does not imply that one variable is causing the other. As a matter of fact, even the most widely cited scientific studies on the relationship between confidence and competence have tended to rely on subjective measures of competence. For example, imagine that we want to examine the correlation between confidence and competence in the domain of sport by asking participants to indicate the degree to which they endorse the following two statements:

Question to assess confidence level → "I am a good sportsman."

Question to assess competence level → "I am a good
    sportsman."

If you see no difference between the above statements, you are
not thinking like an academic—good for you! As common (but not
academic) sense dictates, it is problematic to interpret self-report
statements as indicators of competence. All they represent is re-
spondents' evaluation of their competence, which is, of course, their
confidence speaking.

Relying on a person's self-reports to assess both confidence and
competence creates an illusory correlation: People who evaluate
their confidence highly tend to also evaluate their competence highly,
and vice versa. As psychologist Roy Baumeister, a leading scholar in
self-esteem, noted, "The habit of speaking well of oneself does not
abruptly cease when the respondent turns from the self-esteem
scale to the questionnaire asking for self-report of other behaviors.
People who like to describe themselves in glowing terms will be
inclined to report that they get along well with others, are physically
attractive, do well in school and work, refrain from undesirable actions, and the like."[21]

Carefully designed studies on the relationship between confidence and competence examine objective competence data rather
than relying on people's own accounts of their abilities. Let's look at
a study that psychologist Ed Diener and colleagues did in this vein.[22]
They photographed a bunch of students and asked them to rate
themselves on attractiveness as well as a generic measure of self-
confidence. Students' pictures were then shown to independent
judges, who rated them on attractiveness. The average score given to
a picture by different judges was used as the external, or objective,
measure of attractiveness, independent of participants' self-ratings.

If Dr. Diener and colleagues had followed the methodology employed in most confidence studies, they would have merely correlated participants' self-confidence levels with their self-reported
attractiveness ratings. This correlation was almost .60, suggesting
that being attractive comes with a whopping 80 percent probability
of being confident, and that being unattractive carries an 80 percent
probability of being unassertive. However, when Dr. Diener and his
team correlated participants' confidence levels with their *objective*
attractiveness levels, the correlation was 0, implying that whether
you are attractive or not, your chances of being confident or unconfident are the same: 50 percent. Thus, confident people are attractive only in their own eyes.[23]

The results of Dr. Diener's study have been replicated in many
other domains of competence, such that measuring competence objectively exposes the gap between confidence and competence. This
gap suggests not only that competence and confidence are very different things, but that the underlying reason for the confidence-
competence gap is the disproportionately high number of people
who consider themselves more competent than they actually are,
highlighting one of the most pervasive biases in human thinking:
delusional overconfidence.

Most Confident People Are Deluded

Ask people how good they are at anything, including difficult things
like algebra, and most of them will tell you that they are better than
average, which is logically impossible. How can most people be better than most? The better-than-average bias is caused by our strong

unconscious desire to maintain a positive self-view, a desire most people have. In fact, the only people who are not positively biased in their self-views are those with low confidence. So, if you hardly ever feel that you are better than others, you are actually less delusional than most people.

Strikingly, the better-than-average bias has been found in every domain of competence. For example, most people think their memory is better than average[24] and that they are healthier than average.[25] Most managers view themselves as better-than-average leaders and businesspeople.[26] Professional athletes, such as football players, think they are better than most of their peers,[27] and most people assume their romantic relationships are better than average.[28] In some domains, the better-than-average bias is especially pronounced. For instance, 90 percent of people think they are better drivers than average,[29] 90 percent of high school students think their social skills are better than average,[30] and almost 100 percent of university professors rate their teaching skills as better than average.[31] Of course, some people will be right in thinking that they are better than average, but in most cases this confidence will be unwarranted—it is statistically impossible for 90 or 100 percent to be above average, because by definition the average will fall in the middle of the population rankings.[32] It becomes particularly evident just how wrong these high levels of confidence are when we account for the fact that some of the people who describe themselves as *worse*-than-average may actually be wrong.

In what is arguably the ultimate manifestation of the better-than-average bias, most people see themselves as less biased than the average person.[33] This "bias blind spot" has been documented extensively by Princeton psychologist Emily Pronin. In one of her studies, Dr. Pronin asked participants to estimate the degree to which a range of reasoning biases applied to them, presenting them with nontechnical descriptions of each bias, such as:

> Psychologists have claimed that people show a "self-serving" tendency in the way they view their academic or job performance. That is, they tend to take credit for success but deny responsibility for failure; they see their successes as the result of personal qualities, like drive or ability, but their failures as the result of external factors, like unreasonable work requirements or inadequate instruction.[34]

Upon reading each description, participants estimated how frequently they indulged in each bias compared with the average person. Despite being told how prevalent these biases are, the majority of participants rated themselves as unbiased compared with the overall American population. Dr. Pronin concluded that just because we may know about these self-serving biases and their effects on people's self-views doesn't mean we will realize that we, too, are subject to them:

> Indeed, our research participants denied that their assessments of their personal qualities and their attributions for a particular success or failure had been biased even after having displayed the relevant biases and reading descriptions of them.[35]

The better-than-average bias is best exposed by studies that use objective measures of competence. To this end, my team and I have conducted many large-scale studies correlating people's self-rated and actual abilities. These studies are very straightforward. Participants are asked to rate their own competence (IQ, creativity, math, social skills, etc.) relative to a population average. For example, if they are asked to estimate their own IQ, they are told that the average is 100 and that smart people score 115; extremely smart people, 130; gifted people, 145; etc. After providing their self-evaluations, participants complete an actual test for each of the abilities they rated. Although participants always rate themselves higher than average on all domains, the typical correlation between their self-rated and actual competence is lower than .20, indicating that very few people are able to judge their abilities correctly.

Ignorance Ain't Bliss

The better-than-average bias is just one of dozens of documented biases highlighting the common nature of inflated self-perceptions. In fact, most people distort reality in their favor on a regular basis, because they have such a strong need to see themselves in a positive light. As leading University College London neuroscientist Tali Sharot noted:

> When it comes to predicting what will happen to us tomorrow, next week, or fifty years from now, we overestimate the likelihood of positive events, and underestimate the likelihood of negative events. . . . This phenomenon is known as the optimism bias, and it is one of the most consistent, prevalent, and robust biases documented in psychology.[36]

You may be forgiven for assuming that wishful thinking is a blessing. However, although being able to see the glass as half-full

can help us look forward to the future and approach life with enthu-
siasm, unrealistic optimism impairs our ability to adequately forecast events, preventing us from being properly prepared for the
future. Consider the following examples:

- In the 1960s (as anyone who watches *Mad Men* will notice)
most people were unaware of the fact that smoking tobacco causes
lung cancer. As campaigns started to raise awareness of the harmful effects of tobacco, smoking rates declined substantially. In the
United States, almost one in two adults smoked in 1960; fifty
years later the figure dropped to just one in five. In California,
where antismoking campaigns have been most radical, smoking
rates have dropped lower than anywhere else, and lung cancer incidence is now 25 percent lower than in any other state.[37]

- Knowledge of the adverse effects of lack of exercise and
excessive processed food consumption has led to an increase in
the popularity of fitness programs, organic food, and health
stores over the past ten years.[38] Although these trends are still
subtle, people are now more health conscious than they ever
have been, which will reduce health bills and increase both
quality of life and life expectancy.

- Awareness of our highly destructive pollution levels has
been key to our becoming more environmentally responsible.
When Al Gore's Oscar-winning documentary on climate change
(appropriately named *An Inconvenient Truth*) was released, it
alerted millions of people to a potential man-made catastrophe—
global warming. The message was quite apocalyptic, yet it
helped create a positive change in people's attitudes toward the
environment, increasing recycling and decreasing pollution.

So the truth is often painful, but less painful than ignoring it. It may seem preferable in the short term to be overconfident (whether that relates to phenomena such as health and global warming or to our own abilities), but ultimately, being aware of our own limitations—and, in particular, our defects—can help us reverse and combat their effects.

According to psychological studies, there are few individual benefits associated with optimism or delusional self-confidence. For example, Randall Colvin and his colleagues from the University of California, Berkeley, conducted three psychological studies to examine the effects of overconfidence and inflated self-views on different aspects of competence. In the first of these studies, they estimated self-delusional biases in a sample of 130 eighteen-year-old students (split evenly between men and women) by comparing their self-descriptions with those of independent, trained examiners. For instance, if students regarded themselves as more charming or intelligent than the examiners thought they were, they were deemed overconfident, whereas if the examiners saw the students more favorably than the students saw themselves, they were considered underconfident. Five years later, Dr. Colvin's team tested the same group of students (now age twenty-three) on a wide range of competence criteria, assessed by a new group of independent, trained examiners who were blind to the previous ratings of confidence and competence. Data analyses were carried out separately for women and men, in order to spot potential sex differences in overconfidence (remember that men are usually more confident than women). The results showed that men who self-enhanced at the age of eighteen were described in negative terms by others at the age of twenty-three. For instance, they were likely to be perceived as deceitful, distrustful, and guileful. In contrast, men who did not self-enhance tended to be seen as smart, straightforward, and trusting. So, we can see that self-enhancement handicaps men in their social interactions. As for women, those who self-enhanced at the age of eighteen were regarded as more narcissistic (two common descriptions for them were "sees herself as attractive" and "is a sexual provocateur") at the age of twenty-three. In contrast, women who did not self-enhance were seen by others as interesting, smart, and introspective five years later.[39]

In a second study, Dr. Colvin's team examined the relationship between participants' inflated self-views at the age of twenty-three and how they had been described by friends, acquaintances, and trained examiners at the age of eighteen. Their goal was to identify the typical psychological profile of overconfident participants, and to understand how they were perceived by others. The study revealed that those who self-enhanced at age twenty-three had been viewed much more negatively (compared with those who didn't self-enhance at twenty-three) at age eighteen. Those who self-enhanced at twenty-three had often been described as hostile, and self-enhancing men were also labeled as condescending in their interactions. On the other hand, the twenty-three-year-olds who didn't self-enhance had been viewed much more positively—as sympathetic, considerate, and giving.[40]

In their third and final study, Dr. Colvin and colleagues investigated the short-term consequences of self-delusional biases by comparing how more and less biased participants behave in social interactions. This time, Colvin's team filmed participants—seventy male and seventy female students—and obtained self-ratings of their personalities. In addition, each person was also rated by two other participants, so that researchers could compare their self- and other ratings, as well as how self- and other ratings related to the filmed social interactions. The results were consistent with the two previous studies: For those whose self-evaluations were overly positive, other ratings highlighted undesirable behaviors, portraying those participants in a negative light. Also in accordance with the findings of the previous studies, the participants who did not give overly positive self-evaluations were deemed to have all-round much better social skills. Self-enhancing evaluations, therefore, are not shown to increase social competence, but are in fact detrimental, even if the overly positive self-evaluations do make you feel better about yourself in the short term.[41]

The implications of Dr. Colvin's studies are clear: Contrary to popular belief, overconfidence is more detrimental than underconfidence, and people with inflated self-views are not just deluded but also handicapped in interpersonal relations. In short, robust research evidence categorically contradicts the cliché idea that thinking highly of yourself will make you successful, highlighting a big gap between feeling good and being good.

The Perils of Chasing Confidence

Take a look at these statements:

> "As a Christian, I have no duty to allow myself to be cheated, but I have the duty to be a fighter for truth and justice."
> "I call on you not to hate, because hate does not leave space for a person to be fair and it makes you blind and closes all doors of thinking."
> "It is my greatest wish to enable our people to live with nothing to envy at the earliest possible date, and it is my

greatest pleasure to work energetically, sharing my joys
and sorrows with our people, on the road of translating
my wish into reality."

You may find these quotes inspirational, and there's little doubt
that they would qualify as great moral statements. However, the
first one is by Adolf Hitler, the second one by Saddam Hussein, and
the third by Kim Jong Il. The quotes are far from unusual in that
dictators commonly regard themselves as moral authorities whose
mission is to improve the world; the same is often true of psycho-
paths. A less extreme (and fortunately more harmless) version of
this delusion can be found in the general population. When you ask
the average individual whether she is a good person, and she answers yes, she is usually telling you the truth as *she* sees it. But, as
the preceding quotes suggest, seeing yourself as a nice person and
actually being a nice person are two very different things.

History is not short on examples of famous people who, in a
defensive situation, made use of their persuasive powers in order to
demonstrate their innocence, so much so, they appeared to be lying
to themselves rather than to others. For instance:

When former British prime minister Tony Blair said he had no
regrets about invading Iraq—because he was "pursuing the moral
goal" of getting rid of a dictator—he was probably telling the truth,
but only as *he* saw it or wanted to see it, because the alternative was
to accept that he had made a big mistake. Not only did the Iraq war
cause the death of many innocent people (without improving the
state of international politics); it also compelled Blair to quit politics
altogether, especially when it transpired that the arguments he used
to justify the invasion of Iraq were flawed and based on made-up
evidence.

When Bill Clinton told the American public that he "did not have sex with that woman" (White House intern Monica Lewinsky), he was also telling *his* truth, which could be rationalized by the fact that oral sex may not really qualify as sexual intercourse. Clinton was later forced to admit that he *did* have a relationship with Lewinsky, but only because there was no way he could persuade the American public that he did not have an affair with her—he may have persuaded himself, but nobody else.

Attempts to distort reality are more common among celebrities and politicians than anyone else—after all, they tend to be more narcissistic than average. As Robert Trivers's excellent book *The Folly of Fools* recently highlighted, the most devious and destructive liars are those who are unaware of their own deceit.[42] But does that exempt politicians, the overconfident bankers who enriched themselves while ruining the world economy, or anyone who has acted in a destructive or morally irresponsible way? Not really.

Psychological studies have also highlighted the detrimental effects of self-deception in the general population—the phenomenon does not just apply to politicians, celebrities, and bankers. For instance, an experiment conducted by Kathleen Hoffman Lambird and Traci Mann, two researchers at the University of California, Los Angeles, recruited participants for what was alleged to be an IQ test.[43] After collecting data on participants' self-views, the researchers pretended to administer the IQ test. Upon completing the test, participants were given bogus feedback on their performance—some were randomly selected to receive negative feedback (e.g., "you failed the test"); others were told that they did great. Next, participants were asked to complete the second part of the IQ test. But this time, they had twenty minutes to practice, giving them time to assess their potential for doing well. Hoffman Lambird and Mann then asked participants to estimate how well they would do on the critical trials of the task. The results showed that participants who held less favorable self-views made more accurate predictions of their performance and actually performed better on the test than participants with more positive self-views. Moreover, when participants with favorable self-views were given negative feedback on the first part of the test, they completely overestimated their performance on the second part of the test and performed significantly worse than the rest. This effect was attributed to the defensive nature of the more confident participants: Given that the negative feedback they received was discordant with their positive self-views, they decided to ignore it by reinforcing—and possibly even elevating—their favorable self-views. This fake sense of confidence made them overestimate their performance, and the fact that they did worse on the test shows that they were unable to digest the negative feedback (as they were distracted by it). The implications are that when people defend themselves from adverse experiences by boosting their confidence, they end up not only being in denial, but performing more poorly than they normally would.

In order to test whether defensive high self-views may actually cause people to lie to themselves, Delroy Paulhus, at the University of British Columbia, designed a test to measure what he calls "overclaiming," the tendency to claim knowledge about imaginary or nonexisting topics. This test was administered to participants as a self-reported general knowledge quiz, which asked them to state how much they knew about a list of topics. Given that several of the topics listed were made up (e.g., "cholarine," "ultra-lipid," and "plates of parallax"), Dr. Paulhus and his team were able to compute an over-claiming score for each participant. This score was then correlated with measures of narcissism and deliberate dissimulation (conscious impression management). The results, based on three studies with hundreds of participants, showed that over-claimers tended to be more narcissistic, and they did not engage in deliberate dissimulation; their conscious impression management score was uncorrelated with their over-claiming score. This suggests that rather than misleading or cheating others, overconfident people tend to lie mainly to themselves (the test is completely anonymous, so there is no reason to lie). As Dr. Paulhus and colleagues concluded, "With no audience other than the self, over-claiming is unlikely to be conscious dissimulation: Chronic over-claimers really believe their exaggerated claims of knowledge. . . . This finding supports the view that under low demand conditions, over-claiming has a self-deceptive rather than a controlled origin."[44]

The more confident you are, then, the more likely you are to fool yourself. Back to Tony Blair, Bill Clinton, and the investment bankers behind the latest financial meltdown. . . .

So, given that overconfidence and inflated self-views are so common, you may be wondering why you are not like most people. Why, you may be asking, don't you rate yourself high on different domains of competence or see yourself as more competent than others, as so many people do? The quick, scientifically informed answer is that you are probably more insightful than they are. Indeed, whereas high confidence may result from actual high competence, it is more frequently the product of self-enhancement and reality distortion, an attempt to feel good. Conversely, low confidence tends to result from low competence. That is, more often than not, low confidence signals the capacity to be aware of one's own limitations and competence deficits, and it enables individuals to maintain an accurate representation of reality, even if it's not all that pleasing. In line, there is a gap between feeling and being competent, and that gap can be closed only if you have a realistic understanding of your abilities *or* if you increase your actual competence. Whereas higher confidence tends to make that gap wider, lower confidence tends to reduce it.

The Confidence-Competence Cycle

The following diagram illustrates the Confidence-Competence Cycle, whereby lower confidence is transformed into higher competence.

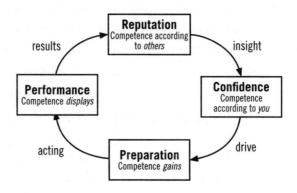

Gaining Competence
The Confidence-Competence Cycle

The details of the diagram will become clearer as you progress through this book, which I hope will help to illuminate the fundamental know-how needed to boost your confidence—that is, knowing that you need to focus on increasing your *competence*. Whether you are keen to boost your career, dating, social, or health confidence, the procedure is always the same: Create visible improvements in your actual ability or state and internalize positive changes in your reputation.

As you gain competence in whichever domain you wish, your performance will help to translate your competence gains into reputation. Thus you consolidate your confidence gains by having your competence recognized by others. This is your end goal. If you get to this stage, your job is done, though you should be careful not to become too complacent. Indeed, if you are too satisfied with your competence (and become too confident), the Confidence-Competence Cycle will begin to reverse. As soon as you feel confident, you will reduce your preparation and stop gaining competence, which makes your performance more reliant on your confidence than on your competence, and your reputation more dependent on faking confidence and competence. The healthier, albeit more resourceful, alternative is to avoid complacency and keep working on your faults and imperfections while maximizing your strengths.

Why Feeling Down Can Be a Good Thing

Many psychological studies show that people with negative self-views are more likely to seek adverse feedback from others than people with positive self-views are. For instance, research shows that less assertive people prefer to interact with people who are critical of them, even when they have the option to spend time with people who praise them. This phenomenon is called "self-affirmation" and reflects a quest for reality that is the exact opposite of the delusional self-enhancement found in people with high confidence and inflated positive self-views. Moreover, the consequences of self-affirmation are in sharp contrast to the consequences of positive self-delusion, such as the optimism or the better-than-average bias. While over-confidence may help you feel good at the expense of being detached from reality, underconfidence may make you feel miserable, but it keeps you focused on reality. Unsurprisingly, negative self-views are more likely to trigger self-improvement than positive self-views are— even in extreme cases of low self-confidence, such as depression.

Have you ever considered the possibility that depression serves an important psychological function? Indeed, it has been argued that from an evolutionary perspective, depression can be understood as an adaptive reaction to real-life problems. For example, depres-sion reduces our interest in trivial matters, which explains one of its key characteristics: the inability to derive pleasure from typically fun and pleasurable activities (e.g., partying, listening to upbeat mu-sic, watching Will Ferrell movies, and even dating). Humans, then, evolved the capacity to be depressed in order to be better equipped to face difficult challenges, especially those requiring high levels of intellectual focus and concentration. Just like fever is our body's at-tempt to coordinate a response to an infection, depression is the brain's attempt to deal with taxing events: the loss of someone we love, the end of a great holiday, or coming to terms with failure or disappointing news. Thus the role of depression is to help us process negative events and ensure that we avoid further blows, by minimiz-ing the probability that we repeat the experiences that triggered depression.[45]

The evolutionary role of depression is in stark contrast to our feel-good society's obsession with medicating its symptoms. In the United States, antidepressants are now the most widely consumed pharmaceutical, and as many as 10 percent of undiagnosed people consume them regularly. Some estimate that antidepressant sales have risen by more than 200 percent in the past twenty years, and many studies show that their consumption generates chronic dependence, causing depression rates to increase almost as much as the consumption of antidepressants. This suggests that people's unwillingness to accept negative self-views and deal with low self-confidence would be disrupting important coping skills that evolved over millions of years to protect us. Have we become too spoiled to deal with unpleasant emotions and failure? As Paul Andrews and Andy Thomson, two psychologists who made a groundbreaking contribution to our understanding of the evolutionary origins of depression, noted: "The current therapeutic emphasis on antidepressant medications taps into the evolved desire to find quick fixes for pain. But learning how to endure and utilize emotional pain may be part of the evolutionary heritage of depression, which may explain venerable philosophical traditions that view emotional pain as the impetus for growth and insight into oneself and the problems of life."[46]

The main philosophical tradition Andrews and Thomson refer to is stoicism, a school of thought that dates back to the ancient Greeks. Unlike the feel-good society, stoicism prescribes the pursuit of truth rather than pleasure. In the words of Lucius Seneca, the most influential Roman stoic: "There is nothing in the world so much admired as a man who knows how to bear unhappiness with courage." According to stoicism, obsessively chasing positive emotions or happiness has self-destructive effects.

Thus, if you are feeling down or lack confidence, don't despair. You are in a good position to begin your self-improvement, if not the *only* position that enables you to do so. There is just one thing you need to remember: Your self-improvement depends not on feeling more *confident*, but on being more competent. In fact, embracing adversity is much more likely to breed self-improvement than is denying it. As a famous anonymous illustration of stoicism suggests, we get stronger through pain, tears, and heartbreak.

The Confidence-Competence Grid

(Closing the Gap Between Feeling and Being Competent)

So, if the goal is to be more competent, how can that be achieved? Contrary to popular belief, the answer is via *low* rather than high confidence. Indeed, whereas high confidence inhibits self-improvement by undermining self-knowledge, low confidence promotes it. More often than not, lower confidence is a symptom of lower competence, telling us that we must improve. You should therefore treasure and embrace your low confidence, as it is a key ingredient of self-knowledge, which in turn is a key ingredient of self-improvement. Unless you know yourself, in particular your weaknesses, you will never get better. Just consider the alternative: lacking competence but feeling confident. As you have probably worked out from the preceding sections, there are few advantages and many disadvantages associated with that profile. The two other possible profiles, namely competence coupled with high confidence, and competence coupled with low confidence, are far less common than the low confidence–low competence and, especially, the high confidence–low competence profiles. In order to visualize the possible links between confidence and competence, let's consider the following figure, which we can refer to as the Confidence-Competence Grid (CCG).

The Confidence - Competence Grid

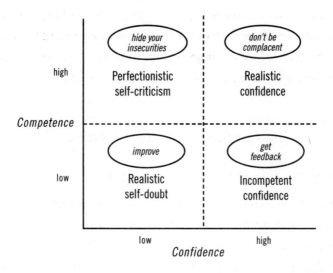

Incompetent Confidence

This is what most confident people have, because their confidence is the product of delusional self-serving biases rather than actual competence. They therefore lack self-knowledge, which implies that they cannot accurately understand how they are seen by others. The biggest problem with this profile is that it causes people to be self-deluded (more on this in the next chapter). If you think that the label of "incompetent confidence" is too harsh, think again. First, these people lack competence. Second, their high confidence exacerbates the negative consequences of low competence—simple example, if you think you can make it across a very busy street on foot without waiting for a break in traffic, you'll get killed (now extrapolate to career, relationships, and other achievement domains and you will understand why so many people end up depressed). Third and

most important, you will never develop knowledge unless you acknowledge what you don't know. The good news for people with incompetent confidence is that they can solve their problem quite
easily by getting feedback from others. Indeed, your levels of competence can be observed by how much confidence *others* have in you,
so if you lack competence but not confidence, you can try to align
your own confidence with other people's confidence in your ability,
which will move you from the bottom right to the bottom left quadrant of the CCG—the realistic self-doubt type. Given that you are
reading this book, I doubt that you meet the criteria for incompetent
confidence, but I figured that you may want to understand what most
people are like. It may come in handy. Whenever you see someone
bragging or showing off, don't assume that they are competent; they
are much more likely to be in the incompetent confidence category.

Realistic Self-doubt

This is a much better alternative to incompetent confidence,
because you are aware of your weaknesses and limitations, which is
crucial if you are planning to improve. In that sense, realistic self-
doubt has two big advantages. First, it is coupled with self-knowledge,
which reflects that you have an accurate understanding of how others see you. Second, it is a motivating force, because being dissatisfied with yourself is the best reason for wanting to improve. There is
also a clear cure for realistic self-doubt, which is to boost your competence. Indeed, although this state is defined by alignment of confidence and competence, it is of course justifiable to break this
alignment by becoming more competent, given that the goal of
being competent is far more important than the goal of being confident. As early as 1896, William James, father of American

psychology, noted that self-esteem could be understood as the ratio of satisfied to unsatisfied goals, such that it could be increased by accomplishing more. The next chapter of this book dwells almost exclusively on this issue, which I'm guessing may be relevant to you, or you wouldn't be reading this book. That said, there's also a chance that you may fall in the top left quadrant, just above realistic self-doubt, namely perfectionistic self-criticism.

Perfectionistic Self-criticism

What happens when you are competent but lack confidence? That's the state of perfectionistic self-criticism—though your accomplishment levels are high, you still lack self-belief. Many exceptional achievers (from professional athletes to accomplished artists to millionaire entrepreneurs) fit this profile, which is why they become exceptional achievers in the first place. Think about it: If you reach the point of being confident about your achievements, why continue to strive for self-improvement or further accomplishments? Interestingly, this type of profile reflects an asymmetry between how others and you evaluate your competence: When you are in a state of perfectionistic self-criticism, you not only regard your competence more unfavorably than others do, but you also tend to think that you are less competent than you really are. It is therefore not unusual for perfectionistic self-critics to compare themselves with more successful individuals, a self-defeating strategy called "upward comparison." In reality, though, the only self-defeating element about this profile is that it promotes one's insecurities, but the effects on competence could not be more beneficial. In fact, when you are your own worst critic, you stand a much better chance of developing competence than when you are your biggest fan. Thus, the only recommendation for this type of profile is to hide your insecurities—something exceptionally successful people do very well. Why is this important? Because even if you are competent, displaying your insecurities to others could encourage them to mistake your low confidence for low competence, particularly when they are incapable of differentiating between confidence and competence, which is often the case.

Realistic Confidence

Finally, the top right quadrant combines high levels of confidence with high levels of competence. This profile represents the logical person's ideal state, and there's nothing wrong with that. However, I should note at the outset that being aware of one's competence incurs the risk of being pleased with oneself first, and then becoming complacent (defined as "a state of uncritical satisfaction with oneself and one's achievements"). The big advice, then, for people with this profile is to avoid being complacent. Otherwise, they may end up falling down to the incompetent confidence quadrant: Stagnation in skill development leads to others becoming better while you rest on your laurels, until you wake up one day and realize that you are not as good as you thought you were (if you ever wake up). Still, there are some advantages associated with this profile. First, it is a state of self-awareness and self-knowledge, which implies that realistic confidence is also linked to a healthy and accurate understanding of what other people think of us. Second, people with this profile are likely to come across as both confident and competent to others. And third, this is the only state in which one can really enjoy the benefits of high confidence—a sense of security and being competent that tastes better than anything else, because it is real.

In short, you can think about a clockwise progression that begins in the incompetent confidence quadrant and ends in the realistic confidence quadrant. Mostly, self-improvement involves closing the gap between confidence and competence, unless you have done so already, in which case you should just try to avoid being complacent— or you will quickly dip to the overconfident region. The two states of alignment of confidence and competence may be seen as the initial and final stages of the process of self-improvement (being in a state of incompetent confidence will rarely trigger improvement). To the extent that you possess self-knowledge, you will have reduced some of the confidence-competence gap already, which will enable you to focus your energies on chasing competence, which, incidentally, should always be the end goal.

Using It:

- The role of confidence in determining success has been exaggerated. We *think* we need higher confidence, but what we really need is to close the gap between our confidence and competence.

- Our culture is turning more and more narcissistic, justifying a blind obsession with feeling good about ourselves. But feeling better about ourselves, and boosting our confidence, will help us achieve nothing until we can also increase our competence to back it up.

- More often than not, confidence does not go hand in hand with competence, because most people have distorted views of themselves. Indeed, most people are biased to think that they are better than average, and are blind to their own biases in making these judgments.

- Optimism and confidence are not helpful if they're unrealistic and blind us to improvements we need to make or dangers we need to avoid.

- Contrary to popular belief, people who are overconfident are less popular with others. Therefore, conveying a more realistic view of your competence will make others view you much more positively and consider you more socially competent than someone who self-enhances.

- Deceiving ourselves into thinking we're better than we really are means that we will overestimate our ability to perform, dismiss negative feedback as inaccurate, and end up doing much worse than if we'd had a realistic self-view.

- Low confidence alerts us to our weaknesses, so lowering our confidence will create the much-needed awareness to improve, and help us close the gap between confidence and competence.

2

Taking Advantage of Low Confidence

When you try to stay on the surface of the water, you sink; but when you try to sink, you float.

Alan Watts (1915–1973)

You Can Benefit from Insecurities

Now that we've started to unravel what confidence is (and isn't), the goal of this chapter is to persuade you of the positive power of low confidence, even in extreme conditions of low confidence such as anxiety and depression. To this end, I'll explain the inherent benefits of low confidence, which include helping you make realistic risk assessments and pushing you to become more competent. As you will see, your insecurities can play an important role in your future success. Indeed, so long as you really want something, you'll find that low confidence is more advantageous than high confidence.

Low confidence is an adaptive tool; it can help you prevent disasters and enhance competence. In order to understand this fully, let us consider the main factors underlying low confidence, which requires first a brief exploration of anxiety.

The evolutionary role of anxiety was to increase our vigilance against and preparation for potential threats by activating the so-called fight-or-flight mechanism. Thus, anxiety is an emotional reaction to perceived danger, which increases levels of worry and attention to it.[1] Even before we could verbalize or put a name to this emotion— before humans developed language—anxiety prepared our body to combat or escape risky situations. So, in response to genuine environmental threats, our ancestors would have experienced anxiety as a call to action (Run!) or *in*action (Don't go there! Be careful! Don't do it!). Such would have been the commands given by anxiety, if it had a voice.

When your confidence is low, and you find yourself in a situation in which you forecast failure (e.g., a college exam, a job interview, a driving test, or a wedding toast), you will experience anxiety and interpret it as a sign that you should try to elude the event. Our brains are prewired to respond automatically to alarming environmental signals (foul smell, noise, bad taste), and this activation is experienced in the form of heightened anxiety.[2] At the same time, the "inner voice" of anxiety is pretty useful. Just imagine how you would end up if you didn't have it at all, especially when you are faced with a tiger or shark.

Unsurprisingly, anxious people are less likely to have fatal accidents. For example, a study of more than a thousand British people found anxiety inclination at the age of fifteen predicted fatal accidents ten years later: The more anxious people had been in their teens (as judged by teachers and valid psychological tests), the less likely they were to have died in accidents by the age of twenty-five.[3] In another study, anxiety was positively related to willingness to enroll in HIV prevention programs. More anxious individuals were more likely to take part in clinical trials to prevent being infected, and were more alert to reporting potential symptoms as well as side effects from the medication.[4] Higher anxiety has also been found to prevent flood-related damage by increasing the likelihood of expecting and preparing for natural disasters. In a study of more than one hundred participants who lived in a flood-prone region, only anxious residents were well equipped to cope with flooding.[5] Heightened anxiety also explains why women tend to outlive men in every culture, despite experiencing the same incidence of illness. Because of their more anxious predispositions, women are more inclined to react to symptoms by arranging visits to the doctor; less likely to drink, smoke, or consume illegal drugs; and less likely to have weight problems.[6] Isaac Marks and Randolph Nesse, psychologists from the Institute of Psychiatry, London, and University of Michigan Medical School, argue that it pays off to react repeatedly to what may turn out to be false alarms, because the cost of this is less than that of failing to respond to a real danger. So anxious responses are therefore common, and serve a much greater purpose—namely, alerting us to danger and helping us to avoid it—than may be evident at first glance. It is for this reason that anxiety disorders are so frequent.[7]

Depression and anxiety disorders, both of which are characterized by very low confidence, are rather common. In the United States, for instance, around 30 percent of the population reportedly suffers from depression or anxiety disorders[8] (and this estimate may be conservative). A recent study of more than forty thousand representative U.S. students found that almost 50 percent of the participants had met the criteria for diagnosable psychiatric illnesses in the previous year, suggesting that real rates of anxiety are much higher than those derived from patients in treatment.[9] There is a strong overlap between anxiety and depression,[10] whereby depression often follows from repeated anxiety episodes—for example, after ongoing fear and worry, people reach a point where they just stop caring (precisely in order to stop feeling anxious and fearful). Although clinical depression is problematic, there are actually advantages to being slightly depressed or having a gloomy outlook on life.

Psychotherapist Emmy Gut proposed that depression originated as an adaptive response for dealing with real problems in the environment, forcing individuals to focus all their attention and energies on dealing with negative events—the opposite of experiential avoidance.[11] As noted by Daniel Nettle, a British evolutionary psychologist, the predisposition to depression carries certain benefits in that people who are negative minded tend to be more self-critical and therefore more competitive: "Having a fairly reactive negative affect system causes people to strive hard for what is desirable and to avoid negative outcomes, and this may well be associated with increased fitness [the evolutionary word for competence]."[12]

Dr. Nettle's argument about the evolutionary benefits of depression is consistent with an abundant body of research demonstrating the higher accuracy of judgment and self-views in people with depressive tendencies, a phenomenon called "depressive realism." Early studies in this area reported that depressive people have a more realistic perception of their reputation, competence, and social status than nondepressed individuals.[13] These results have since been replicated widely, especially in people with mild pessimistic tendencies.

Ultimately, low confidence is an adaptive risk management strategy, which reflects your interpretation of your past, present, and future competence. It is less biased when it matches your reputation (or how others view your competence), and more biased in the case of perfectionistic self-criticism, when you rate your competence lower than others do. However, even when biased, low confidence is advantageous in that it keeps losses to a minimum. Moderate pessimism has an important adaptive value, as illustrated by psychiatrist Robert Leahy with a metaphorical card game, in which a pessimist and an optimist place bets on the game. As you might expect, each time, the pessimist bets that he will lose and then drops out, and the optimist bets that he will win. Following this strategy, the pessimist will not accumulate any winnings, but will only ever lose a certain fixed amount. The optimist, on the other hand, leaves his outcome ultimately up to chance—he may win a lot of money, but equally he stands to lose everything, and eventually this is what will happen. Leahy argues, however, that "few pessimists will stay this negative forever and, perhaps through some adaptive impulsivity, may play a hand. . . . This may lead to some winnings, breaking some of the inflexibility of the pessimism."[14]

Or, if you prefer an analogy about the animal kingdom instead of a card game: "While a grazing deer that lifts its head every few seconds to scan for predators has less time to eat, mate, and care for offspring, one that lifts its head too little may eat more, but is at greater risk of being eaten itself."[15] Thus anxiety and low confidence are adaptive in that they help you to err on the side of caution and minimize losses.

The main purpose of low confidence is therefore to help you adapt to the environment. When low confidence triggers anxiety, it serves the goal of protecting you—anxiety is just the reminder that you need to pay attention to your low confidence and perhaps work to increase your competence. At the same time, your confidence can be low because you have a generic tendency to expect negative outcomes—that is, a pessimistic bias. Indeed, some people are generally less confident, more anxious, and more negative than others. All these characteristics are part of the same syndrome and coexist because of early childhood anxieties as well as inherited predispositions. Either way, low confidence fulfills an adaptive role, which is to promote a loss-minimization strategy. Whether you are just feeling temporarily unassertive because you think you won't succeed at something, or you have a general pessimistic and self-critical outlook, which tends to default on catastrophic predictions of the future, low confidence is your mind's attempt to prevent disasters and protect you.

Low Confidence Protects You

You feel anxious and worried when you are lacking confidence, so you pay attention to important adaptive signals and inhibit your behavior. And yet, our narcissistic world has persuaded us to look at low confidence as a drag. We don't think of its causes or consequences; we focus instead on the uncomfortable feelings and thoughts it evokes: worry, tension, anxiety, and even panic. But these sensations have a purpose, namely to prevent negative outcomes. The following examples may illustrate this functional element of realistic low confidence:

1) You are invited to give a presentation on a topic you don't know that well.

I am often invited to speak about things I don't know much about. Although I tend to decline now, in my earlier career years I normally defaulted to "yes" regardless of the offer. A few years ago I was asked to give a lecture on "shoe psychology" (how your shoe preferences reflect important aspects of your personality). Given that I had done a bit of work on the psychology of advertising, I accepted the invitation and looked forward to giving the talk. But the time of the talk approached and I started worrying about what I was going to say. Not only had I never done any work on the psychology of shoe preferences; I needed to fill a one-hour slot on the subject. The audience—as I came to realize only a couple of weeks before the talk—included a mix of fashion designers, businesspeople, marketing and advertising executives, and psychologists who actually specialized in the subject. I was feeling nervous and totally unconfident. Was my low confidence warranted? For sure. Would it have been better to feel confident? Most certainly not, except for the fact that it is unpleasant to feel anxious and to lack confidence. These feelings helped me realize that unless I prepared, I was destined to fail and embarrass myself in front of an audience of professionals. So I spent many hours and various days in the library, reading everything I could find about shoe preferences and psychology, and I prepared enough to give a one-hour talk on the subject. The presentation was fine in the end, but if it weren't for my low confidence and anxiety, it would have been disastrous and embarrassing. This was just one of many times I have been grateful to my low confidence for pushing me to prepare for my lectures.

2) Someone fiercer than you provokes you into an argument.

Do you want to know how to avoid losing the fight? Don't take on people who are stronger than you. And in order to achieve this you will need the ability to realize that you will lose the argument—that is, you will need to lack confidence in your ability to win. Whether you are at school, at a bar, or at work, your low confidence helps you avoid battles that would end with your defeat. Although we don't think about them often, there are many situations in which beating your fears will enhance the probability of being beaten (psychologically, emotionally, or even physically). If your confidence is trying to tell you that you should not do something, then you probably shouldn't. This applies not just to fights—verbal or physical—between two people, but also to sporting combats. In boxing, for instance, the reigning champion needs to decide very carefully if it is worth risking his or her title by fighting a contender. The same applies to war. Would America have gone to Vietnam, Iraq, or Afghanistan if it had felt less confident about winning those wars? Would America invade Iran if it felt more confident about its chances to win there? Probably. Just as low confidence prevents you from getting beaten, high confidence leads you to underestimate your rival and be beaten by him. This principle is captured nicely in *The Art of War*, Sun Tzu's famous book on military strategy:

> If you know the enemy and know yourself, you need not fear the result of a hundred battles. If you know yourself but not the enemy, for every victory gained you will also suffer a defeat. If you know neither the enemy nor yourself, you will succumb in every battle. [16]

3) You are gambling in a Las Vegas casino and you are "feeling lucky."

Guess why most gamblers go bankrupt. Because they cannot stop gambling despite the fact that the odds are against them. And when they lose, they interpret their losses as "near wins" in order to justify and maintain their high confidence.[17] If only they felt a bit less confident about their chances of winning, they would quit before it was too late. This next-time-lucky mentality is also found in gambling varieties manifested outside the casino, such as financial investment. There is now wide agreement about the fact that the 2008 economic crisis could have been prevented if such vacuous investments hadn't been made on the basis of overconfidence. Anne Sibert, an Icelandic economist who investigated the causes of the financial crash in her country (where the global crisis was kick-started), attributed this overconfidence to a specific feature in the brain chemistry of male traders: "An investor may buy into a known bubble so long as he reckons it will continue into the next period. He counts on his ability to time the market and sell the asset before the bubble pops. The research suggests making money off a bubble in the early stages inflates male overconfidence, and this feeds the bubble's growth."[18] In line, Dr. John Coates and Professor Joe Herbert, from the University of Cambridge neuroscience department, found that on very successful days, traders display higher levels of testosterone, which increases their confidence and risk taking in subsequent investments.[19] Given men's biological predisposition to be blinded by greed, it may not be a bad idea to have more female traders. Not only do women have lower levels of testosterone; they are also more risk averse and less overconfident than men, which is why they have fewer traffic accidents and are rarely found drunk driving (especially compared to men).

Many of the borrowers who ended up defaulting on mortgages that seemed too good to be true may not have borrowed as much money if they hadn't experienced a false sense of security, and if they had felt less confident about their ability to make monthly payments. And if you think that excess of confidence played a role only in the *latest* financial crisis, think again. Just before the big economic crash of 1929, President Calvin Coolidge asserted that we could be optimistic about the future.[20] Last year alone, JPMorgan Chase disclosed a two-billion-dollar trading loss, which came as a total surprise to investors. The common explanation for these and other gambling disasters is that when most people bet on something (e.g., a horse, a roulette number, or Facebook stock), they automatically increase their belief that the event will occur, because they would feel stupid and worry otherwise. The implications are clear: Low confidence helps us question our competence, which will minimize our losses, even at the level of extreme economic meltdowns.

4) You are tempted to cheat on your romantic partner.

Most people will at some point have the experience of being strongly sexually attracted to someone while in a romantic relationship with someone else. This temptation is more common for some people than others, and there are even stronger differences between people's ability to resist it. One of the reasons why people choose not to pursue extramarital affairs is that they are afraid of being caught. Low confidence warns them that they may not have the competence to get away with the deceit. Other people go ahead because they feel confident that they won't be found out. This is why infidelity is so prominent among overconfident, powerful people. Can you guess what John Edwards, Paul Wolfowitz, Randall Tobias, and David Petraeus have in common? They are all prominent politicians or military officers who were caught in extramarital affairs. The link between power and infidelity is also evident among top executives, such as HP's boss Mark Hurd and Boeing's boss Harry Stonecipher, both of whom lost their jobs because of cheating scandals.

It would seem that the saying "Power corrupts" is as applicable to relationships as it is to monetary matters. In a recent large-scale psychological study, Dr. Joris Lammers and colleagues, from Tilburg University,[21] investigated the relationship between power and romantic infidelity. They argued that power increases the likelihood of cheating because powerful people are less likely to be deterred by the potential risks associated with cheating. Their overconfidence will typically lead them to underestimate the riskiness of the situation (the probability of getting caught) as well as its negative consequences (the probability that getting caught will ruin their relationship or career).

As you can see, confidence plays a big role in the relationship between power and cheating. Power makes people feel more confident, and their confidence makes them underestimate the risks and consequences of cheating, denigrate their partner, and believe that they can easily replace him or her with someone else. To test whether this relationship held true in the general population, Lammers and colleagues tested more than twelve hundred adults from their native Netherlands in 2011. Their sample included people employed in all strata of society and occupations, from fairly unskilled and poorly paid jobs to powerful corporate positions. The authors found the expected relationship between confidence and infidelity: The more confident people were, the more they reported an intention to cheat on their partners. Once again, a lack of confidence is associated with an important benefit, namely the ability to maintain a faithful relationship.

If people were less confident about their ability to have affairs without being caught and to replace their partner with another desirable partner, there would be fewer acts of romantic infidelity. Lower confidence is therefore an advantage—it helps us refrain from making stupid decisions. This explains why so many celebrities and people in positions of extreme power are caught having affairs and why, even when they have some of the most recognizable faces on the planet, they are still certain that nobody will ever find them out. Exceptional achievers who claim that extraordinary confidence is the secret of their success are more often its victims.

As you can see, low confidence has many important benefits. At an individual level, it can prevent financial bankruptcy, relationships breakups, career failure, and premature death. At a population level, it prevents severe economic crises and wars.

Low Confidence Helps You Improve

Have you ever been in an extreme situation? Have you ever seen a close friend or relative in danger, or been so incensed by something that you felt the urge to bring justice? Have you ever *really wanted* something? If you have, then look back at any of those experiences and you will realize that confidence is much more trivial than most people think. There is an obvious reason for that: So long as you really want something, your confidence won't stop you from trying to attain it, and if you don't care about something, your confidence won't be of any help anyway. Furthermore, if you are absolutely determined to pursue a goal, high confidence will be more problematic, because the more certain you feel about the likelihood of getting what you want, the less you will work to get it. Conversely, thinking that your goal is hard to achieve will make you work more to attain it, unless you are not really serious about your goal. Think about it: Wanting to be good at something is incompatible with thinking you are good at something.

Some of the most competent people I know are less confident than the average person. Most of the highly confident people I have met are less competent than the average person. Although I rarely feel successful, I am probably quite competent in my profession. If

I were *more* confident, I would be less competent, because I would lack that additional drive that my lower confidence (which signals a need to improve competence) provides. It's important to recognize that low confidence does not stop you from trying to achieve what you want. If you really want something, feeling that you lack the competence to attain it will only make you work harder, and hard work—not confidence—is the essence of achievement.

Achievement can be broken down into two parts: preparation and performance. When you perform, confidence is advantageous because it enhances others' perceptions of your competence and distracts you from your inner insecurities. Conversely, when you are performing in low-confidence mode your inner doubts distract you, making you lose focus on the task and conveying to others that you lack competence. However, performance is only a small part of the achievement equation, amounting to just 10 percent of the time and effort needed to accomplish something. The remaining 90 percent consists of preparation, and the less confident you are about your performance, the more motivated you should be to prepare. Think about being told you have to give an important presentation. You might hate feeling unconfident and anxious, but these feelings will motivate you to prepare more in order to avoid failure or embarrassment, and therefore will ultimately mean your presentation is much more of a success than if you had not worried and seen no need to prepare as much. Thus, low confidence is not a bad state in which to begin your self-improvement program: Feeling more confident is rather useless until you gain competence, and low confidence helps you gain competence. In other words, successful change is the product of greater effort, which is much more likely to result from under-confidence than from overconfidence.

This commonsense argument is not just the logical way to think about low confidence; it is also consistent with the most influential theories of motivation and based on well-established scientific facts. The eminent psychologist Albert Bandura (famous for coining the term *self-efficacy*, which has been the preferred academic word for self-confidence since the 1980s) postulated that high competence leads to high confidence. In line, boosting performance—"mastery achievement"—is the most effective method of increasing confidence. Indeed, here's what the evidence indicates:

- Clinical interventions designed to eliminate addictions and overcome psychological and physical health problems (e.g., overeating, smoking, drinking, gambling) indicate that higher levels of confidence are advantageous only when they result from previous increases in actual competence, which means that *competence* gains, not confidence gains, are the decisive factor.[22] For example, if you persuade smokers that they are able to quit smoking, confidence alone won't lead to anything, but if smokers manage to first reduce their smoking habits, they will experience a justifiable sense of confidence that will translate into further competence gains.

- Lower confidence has been found to increase resource allocations (i.e., investment of more time and energy in trying to accomplish a goal)[23] and competence, as described by William Powers.[24] Studies that manipulate participants' confidence levels by giving random feedback on their performance (a common methodology) show that lowering people's confidence motivates them to work harder on their competence,[25] whereas increasing their confidence has the opposite effect. For example, Dan Stone, from the University of Illinois,[26] found that high confidence leads people to overestimate their abilities, which in turn causes them to be less attentive and effortful than their less confident counterparts.

- The most solid scientific theories of motivation, such as perceptual control theory,[27] argue that motivation results from the perceived discrepancy between present states and desired states.[28] Since higher confidence reduces this discrepancy and lower confidence increases it, lower confidence is a stronger motivational force than higher confidence. In other words, as your confidence increases, the gap between your perceived competence and your goals narrows, leading to a decrease in effort levels. Your confidence is like a thermostat that senses the likelihood of attaining a desired level of performance. Like any other thermostat, it signals a reduction of effort when the end goal is attained. Higher confidence will signal this reduction sooner than lower confidence.

As we can see, there is a wealth of research evidence suggesting that lower confidence is an important driver of change, and that it causes future competence gains. While higher competence produces confidence gains, the process begins when one successfully identifies the need to invest more time and effort to achieve a goal (and this results from low, not high, confidence). The paradoxical nature of confidence is that higher confidence may increase people's aspirations while decreasing their dedication. If you feel you are competent, you will be more likely to have more ambitious goals *and* believe that they are easier to attain, which will reduce your levels of focus and effort. On the other hand, if your confidence is low, you may have less ambitious goals, but you will also be more likely to perceive them as challenging, which will incentivize you to prepare more and allocate more time and energy to attaining them. Accordingly, you are more likely to capitalize on your insecurities than on your assertiveness, and you can continue building upon those successes, so long as you don't get complacent. Security, on the other hand, calls for coasting (a natural deceleration); insecurity calls for power and acceleration.

Being Other Focused

It may be comforting to assume that others care about what we think and feel, as if we were the main characters of a reality TV show—this is why so many people spend many hours a day tweeting or updating their Facebook status. Likewise, we often assume that others can tune in to our thoughts and emotions. When we are upset, we expect everybody else to be upset. When we are certain about something, we expect others to be equally certain and agree with us; when they don't, we almost inevitably argue. In reality, however, the only person who really cares about what you think is you. This may sound harsh and be hard to digest, but it shouldn't. In fact, coming to terms with the idea that your thoughts and feelings are interesting mainly to you will be hugely advantageous for your interactions with others; it will stop you from being self-obsessed. In this world, there are two types of battles—the one you fight against others and the one you fight against yourself. Of these two battles, only the former can be won. The battle against yourself will not only end up in defeat, but it will also wear you out and stop you from winning battles against others. What I'm trying to say is that you should stop focusing on yourself and start focusing on others. My advice is based on simple reasoning that is in line with what we have learned about confidence and competence so far:

> Self-focus = worrying about your confidence
> Other focus = worrying about your competence

In order to get better, you need to get others to believe in you. In fact, if you have always had low confidence you are probably your own harshest critic, so persuading others that you are competent may be easier than it seems. I know many people who are riddled with self-doubt and have confidence problems, when common sense would dictate that they shouldn't—they are talented, charming, and successful people. Yet they get too fixated on their own thoughts, instead of focusing on what other people think about them. If you focus too much on your own feelings, you will end up worrying about your confidence instead of focusing on your competence. If you pay attention just to yourself, you won't have time to pay attention to others; if, on the other hand, you pay attention to others (which, admittedly, includes what they think of you), you will be able to succeed in social interactions and more. Remember, it's the rule, not the exception, that we are self-focused, so if you act interested in others, they will think you are special.

I recently helped interview some job candidates for a bank. The CEO of the bank was chairing the selection panel. He was obviously very self-focused. His confidence was such that he didn't acknowledge anybody else's existence unless they paid attention to him. Three of the job applicants interviewed extremely well; they were sharp and eloquent, and had impeccable credentials. However, they failed to pay attention to the CEO. Being confident, they talked so much about themselves that the CEO barely managed to say a word. The last candidate interviewed poorly. He was nervous and hesitant, and struggled to articulate a proper answer to most questions. As he didn't speak much, the CEO had a great opportunity to talk about himself, his business, his reputation, and how important his contribution to the world was. The candidate just nodded. Guess who got the job. That's right, the weaker interviewee, who gave the CEO an opportunity to talk about himself and expressed his admiration for him.

William James famously stated that the most fundamental principle governing human behavior is the universal craving for others' appreciation. Learn to appreciate others—even if it means faking an interest in them—and they will like you. As Dale Carnegie, the most successful self-help author of all time, wrote: "Of course, you are interested in what you want. . . . The rest of us are just like you: we are interested in what we want. So the only way on earth to influence other people is to talk about what *they* want and show them how to get it."[29] In a similar vein, Henry Ford noted that the single most important secret to success is the ability to understand the other person's viewpoint and see things from other people's perspectives— what psychologist usually refer to as "empathy." If most people fail at this, it is because they are too fixated on themselves, and that is true for both people with high and those with low confidence. Overconfident people ignore the fact that others don't find them competent; underconfident people ignore the fact that they do. Both of them are focused on themselves, so much so that they have little time to understand how other people see them.

Given the discussion at hand, I'd like to share with you the best piece of advice I have ever been given: "Tomas, it's not all about you." Although in the moment this feedback was painful—because it revealed how narcissistic my behavior was—it helped me realize that I was spending a great deal of time talking and thinking about myself, which made it quite difficult for me to focus on other people. People with low confidence tend to make the same mistake: They are so concerned about their own self-esteem that they ignore the concerns of other people. During face-to-face interactions with others, we tend to notice people's self-obsession only when they seem overconfident and self-important. However, start analyzing people's written communications (e-mails, letters, messages, etc.) and you will easily spot individuals who are self-centered and self-obsessed. Just count the number of times people use the words *I* or *me* when they communicate with others (this is a common research technique to spot narcissists). You can even do it for yourself. Keep this in mind next time you write an e-mail, and you will see how hard it is to avoid these words—but it pays off.

The good news is that if you do manage to avoid talking about yourself you will be forced to pay attention to others and see the world from their perspective, which will help you overcome your insecurities. Our insecurities are only exacerbated if we pay too much attention to ourselves. I hope you are starting to see that how *you* feel about you is less important than you think. The crucial thing in life is how others think of you, and that is a function not of your confidence, but of your competence.

Successful People Are Rarely Themselves

Successful people are hardly ever themselves, because they hide their insecurities. Success depends on having the repertoire of skills necessary to avoid being yourself, which is a key requirement for presenting yourself in a desirable way to others. Your insecurities about how you should interact with others make your interactions with others successful; they are a sign that you care about other people, and you should not ignore them. As the great personality psychologist Robert Hogan noted, social skills are what you need in order to effectively translate your character (the person you want to be) into your reputation (the person you are). The only people who are themselves are people with no social skills, and they are rarely successful. Make every possible effort to disguise your natural you, whoever that may be, and portray the best possible version of yourself to others—you will reap the benefits.

Although we often think of exceptional achievers as genuine people, the truth is very different from this urban legend. Instead of being themselves, successful people tend to create attractive reputations, which means that they are good at getting others to think highly of them.

Bill Gates has been the richest person in the world for most of the past decade. Did you ever ask yourself what drives Mr. Gates? He started as a Harvard dropout, which suggests that he had a rebellious attitude toward his parents and authority. Let's face it, most people who are given the chance to go to Harvard will work hard to make the most of that wonderful opportunity, which will open all sorts of doors for the rest of their lives. He went on to create Microsoft, which made him a prototype for the computer nerd turned entrepreneur we now know so well. That reputation was soon replaced by one of a ruthless businessman who created and exploited one of the biggest monopolies in modern history. Clearly, one does not get to that stage without being insanely driven, and the latest twist in Mr. Gates's career suggests that he is primarily motivated by the need to be loved by others. Indeed, after becoming the youngest self-made billionaire in history (a title that now belongs to Mark

Zuckerberg, the founder of Facebook) and subsequently becoming the richest person on the planet, Gates decided to give most of his fortune away to philanthropic causes. While this is no doubt a wonderful act, it should also be interpreted in the context of his wider biography. His desire to do good is inspired by his relentless drive for acceptance and need for recognition, which would not exist without some insecurities.

Like Bill Gates, most successful people succeed at hiding their insecurities, which is why we tend to be so surprised when, unlike Bill Gates, they confess that they are riddled by self-doubt. There are many cases of well-known people who have confessed to being insecure despite being widely regarded as "confidence icons" of modern society. Johnny Depp, actor and modern-day sex symbol known for his daring and creative performances, has admitted that despite his fame and popularity, his self-esteem is still not particularly high.[30] Singer Robbie Williams, one of the most successful pop stars of the nineties, has said that his apparent confidence is in actuality just a mask for his nerves.[31] A third example is the actress Demi Moore, who has expressed her deep insecurities that she will come to the end of her life to find that she was never really lovable.[32]

The clearest proof of the importance of creating a good impression on others is how horribly wrong things go when people stop making an effort to portray themselves positively and decide instead to be themselves. Consider the many cases of reputational suicide we've seen committed: John Galliano, for example, one of the most respected fashion designers in the world, whose alcohol-fuelled anti-Semitic rants at strangers in Paris ruined his reputation and career. Although Galliano blamed his behavior on the booze and drugs he had consumed, he was really just being himself.

The list of celebrities who have ruined their reputations by "being themselves" is endless, and also includes women: Consider Britney Spears, who went from angelic pop princess to crystal-meth junkie, and Whitney Houston, whose transition was even more destructive. However, celebrities aren't the only ones who need to work hard to avoid being themselves. The recent explosion of social networking sites, such as Twitter and Facebook, has highlighted the importance of maintaining a positive digital reputation: Many employers and recruiters are now snooping on their employees' and job applicants' social media profiles to get a better sense of who they are dealing with, and rightly so. If recruiters and employers were granted full access to people's Facebook accounts, most Facebook users would be unemployed.

By doing what society dictates, we successfully manage to avoid being ourselves, and this is especially true for exceptional achievers.

If You Fake It You'll Make It

There is no doubt that people who come across as confident enjoy a wide range of social benefits . . . so long as they are also seen as competent! People who display competence are considered more charming, charismatic, leader-like, and even more physically attractive. The social rank conferred by these things encourages even more people to get along with them. When someone is seen as successful by others, we want to be liked by that person in order to elevate our own social status. But these people may just be faking confidence. In fact, their success depends on how we see them—they owe it to us.

Conversely, there is no evidence that how confident you feel *inwardly* has any effect on how people perceive you—people can only observe your behavior; they have no insight into how you feel.

In line, unless you can project your confidence externally, so that it spills over to your observable behaviors, few people will be aware of it. Other people don't know what you think, unless you make no effort to conceal it. In general, they can only see what you do, and, at best, speculate about how you feel or what you think. Your inner confidence is invisible, but your competence has a very visible element; it is on this that others judge your abilities.

The famous "fake it till you make it" cliché is not a bad piece of advice. If you can fake it, then you can fool other people into thinking that you are competent, which will result in positive feedback, and in turn, a deserved confidence boost—even if you think you don't deserve it. So, you may have internal insecurities to begin with, but if you can fool others into thinking that you are competent (we'll learn more about specific areas of competence in the following chapters), they will reward you with the illusion of competence. And the illusion, frankly, is as good as the real thing, because what other people think of you is what matters after all.[33]

But how difficult is it to fool others? Not difficult at all . . .

Psychologists have conducted hundreds of studies on faking, assessing both people's ability to deceive and their accuracy in detecting lies told by others. A typical study involves 40 judges independently deciding whether 15 different statements, each delivered by a different person, are true or false. The average duration of each statement is 50 seconds; all are filmed and shown to all judges. In a review of decades of research in this area, Drs. Charles Bond Jr. and Bella DePaulo summarized the results of more than 200 studies comprising data for almost 25,000 participants.[34] So, what do the results show? The success rate for spotting truths is a bare 53 percent; the success rate for spotting lies is a bare 47 percent. Therefore, our accuracy for spotting honest answers is just 3 percent better than chance, and our accuracy for detecting lies is 3 percent worse than chance, so we would achieve more or less the same degree of accuracy by flipping a coin; lies can barely be distinguished from the truth.

You may be thinking that these results could simply reflect the fact that some people are much better liars than others. For instance, if some people are found out 75 percent of the time (because they are terrible liars) and others just 25 percent (because they are expert liars), these two opposite types of deceivers would "cancel each other out" and result in an average 50 percent success rate for all judges. That's not the case. There is compelling scientific evidence for the fact that every person is perfectly capable of deceiving others, which is consistent with the idea that lying is an adaptive and socially rewarded behavior. As Bond and DePaulo point out, we all tell lies on a daily basis—to please people and to save face. Mostly our lies are to preserve our reputations; accordingly, "the signs of deception are subtle, and social norms encourage people to accept others' representations at face value."[35]

Despite the fact that society preaches honesty, we are trained to lie, even as kids. Dr. Kang Lee, the director of the Dr. Eric Jackman Institute of Child Study, at the University of Toronto, classifies children's lies into three main categories: 1) lies that enables them to get along with others, by being kind (e.g., "You are very pretty," "Your cake was delicious"); 2) lies that protect them from potential punishment (e.g., "It wasn't me," "I didn't know you wanted me to do that"); and 3) self-deceiving lies ("I am a good boy," "I never lie"). As adults, we continue to rely on these three types of lies. The first two are indicative of social adjustment; that is, we have learned to utilize these types of lies appropriately to get by in society. Furthermore, there is an evolutionary basis for deceiving others: Our ancestors benefited from faking aggression and strength to threaten potential rivals and predators, especially when running away was not an option. All this indicates that more competent people are able to lie when needed, and that part of their success may be owed to deceiving others rather than themselves. Yet as the great Abraham Lincoln famously noted, it is possible to fool some individuals all the time and all individuals some of the time, but it's not feasible to fool all individuals all the time. Therefore, rather than just improving how you present to others, it is important that you also focus on genuinely becoming more competent. Chapters 4 through 7 explain how you can achieve this with regard to your career, social and romantic relations, and health.

Using It:

- Low confidence pushes you to become more competent.

- Anxiety can be beneficial by alerting you to danger so you can avoid it.

- If you lack confidence in your abilities, you'll be motivated to work harder for what you want to achieve, and you'll be more likely to increase your competence as a result.

- Taking an interest in others and their perspectives, as well as being more focused on other people and less on yourself, will help you understand how others see you and help you overcome your insecurities.

- Present the best version of yourself to others. It's not difficult to fool other people, and displaying competence will have a great effect on how others perceive you, even if in your own mind you feel insecure.

3

Reputation Is King

I go eyeball to eyeball with some other creature—and I yearn to know the essential quality of its markedly different vitality. . . . Give me one minute—just one minute—inside the skin of this creature . . . and then I will know what natural historians have sought through the ages. . . . Instead, we can only peer in from the outside, look our subject straight in the face, and wonder, ever wonder.   —Stephen Jay Gould (1941–2002)

It is easy to understand the frustration of paleontologist Stephen Jay Gould: No matter how hard we try, it's impossible to know for certain what other people are thinking or feeling. Sure, there are times when we may be able to guess, but guessing and knowing are different things.

When a movie makes you cry, your tears are triggered by posed emotional displays from the actors. Their emotions seem as genuine as your own, but they aren't. Likewise, there is a difference between being and seeming confident. Although others will try to detect your true confidence level via the signals you send, they can only build an impression from the cues you provide. Thus your confidence has two faces. The first is the internal face, or how able you think you are. The second is the external face, or how able other people think that you think you are.

But why do people care about others' levels of confidence? For the same reason you care about your own: to better predict future outcomes and improve your decisions. For example, assessing your job confidence may help you decide whether you should accept a new work assignment and how much effort it would require. By the same token, assessing colleagues' job confidence may help you decide whether you will be able to rely on them for help. When you already know your colleagues, you won't need to rely on their confidence as much, but when you have to assess the competence of strangers—in the absence of knowledge of their actual competence— you will look for confidence signs.

Think about the first time you are introduced to someone. You try to work out whether they are good at X, Y, or Z; you go about this by assessing how confident they are in those or related domains of competence. If the person says she is a good swimmer, you will also assume that she is sporty, healthy, and perhaps even happy. However, you are making these judgments based on her reported swimming skills. Likewise, if someone tells you he went to a prestigious university, you will assume that he is smart, successful, and perhaps rich—but your inferences would be based primarily on his reported competence. Whatever inferences you end up making, it is clear that your intention is to evaluate his competence, not his confidence, even though you assess his confidence in order to work out how competent he is. If you know that someone tends to be extremely confident, you might learn to deduct points from her competence claims, and knowing that someone is underconfident will make you do the opposite. Remember, even if we could accurately assess how confident others feel, that would hardly inform us of their actual competence, not least because the vast majority of confident people are less competent than they think.

There are reasons to believe that humans are biologically predisposed to confuse confidence with competence. Our evolutionary ancestors may have been less able to fake emotions than we are, which made confidence a good proxy for competence. Charles Darwin famously argued that our emotions developed for the purpose of communicating information relevant to the survival of our species. When a member of the same clan spotted a predator, an anxious reaction alerted his clan to the danger before they even saw it, enabling them to prepare. In line, members of a species capable of expressing emotions to others in the group would outlive a species that lacked that capability—the predator would eat *them* first. There was also a likely competitive advantage to expressing positive emotions, namely to signal strength, power, and safety to other clan members as well as to rival species. When our ancestors succeeded at hunting or mating, they displaycd cmotions that conveyed competence. When they failed, they communicated those failures and their weaknesses via relevant emotions, too.[1] Thus millions of years ago there was no difference between confidence and competence: Confidence was just the observable manifestation of competence.

But there are also clear evolutionary drawbacks to openly expressing emotions. When the predator is someone who can spot your anxiety and use it against you, you are better off hiding your fears than displaying them. If your rivals perceive you as competent, they will be less likely to fight you and more likely to respect you, and they will pick on a seemingly weaker target. Survivors were therefore those who were successful in displaying high levels of confidence, even if this was not a true reflection of their competence. Being able to hide your emotions is evolutionarily advantageous, and it pays off in everyday interactions with others . . . unless they find you out. Furthermore, when bluffing becomes quite common, it is not that easy to persuade others of the fact that you are competent when in fact you are not.

In this chapter, we'll establish the fact that confidence is valuable to other people only if it is accompanied by competence. I'll also highlight the importance of reputation—your competence according to others. More often than not, what other people think of you matters, regardless of whether they are right. Thus, in order to close the gap between confidence and competence, it is important to understand how others see you; boosting your competence is relevant only when other people notice it.

If Character Is Destiny, Reputation Is Fate

Although we tend to use *fate* and *destiny* interchangeably, fate is actually more inevitable than destiny. People also use *reputation* and *character* synonymously, but *character* tends to refer to your identity and how you view yourself, whereas *reputation* is your character according to others. Of course, neither our character nor our reputation explains everything we do. Humans are fairly unpredictable, and no psychologist or futurologist can accurately forecast what we will do next. At the same time, we are creatures of habit, and our habits are better reflected in our reputation than in our character. This follows logically from the facts that (a) our character is shaped by reputation more than vice versa (as explained in the previous chapter), and (b) it is easier to assess one's own reputation than character (given how biased most people's self-views are). Consider the following:

Drs. Brian Connelly and Deniz Ones compared the accuracy of reputation and character in predicting future behavior, including key aspects of competence, such as overall college and work performance and relationship success. Their results, based on hundreds of independent studies comprising thousands of participants, show that for every domain examined, reputation was a more accurate predictor of people's competence than their self-views were.

Across a wide range of key competence domains, then, our self-perceptions are less realistic indicators of our competence than are others' perceptions of us, which probably doesn't surprise you by now. This is especially true when it comes to judging elements of our character that are closely related to competence. For instance, others' assessments of how calm and emotionally balanced we are predict the impression we make on strangers far better than our own assessment of our calmness and emotional balance does. Others' views of our leadership potential, creativity, self-management skills, and work ethic are a much more accurate predictor of our future job performance than our own assessments of those traits. And others' views of our self-discipline, emotional calmness, and social skills are a much better predictor of our subsequent academic achievement than our self-assessments of those traits.

Connelly and Ones's investigation focused on adults, but the same pattern of results emerges in adolescents and children. For example, my colleague Denis Bratko and I investigated the relationship between character and reputation in secondary school pupils. We assessed character via self-reports of personality, and reputation by asking classmates (pupils who had sat next to them for at least one year) to provide ratings of the same traits. As in samples of adults, character and reputation were related but different—with a 20 to 30 percent overlap between pupils' self-views and their classmates'

views of them. In line with Connelly and Ones's findings, reputation was a better predictor of pupils' competence—their actual
school performance—than pupils' self-views. Indeed, even after pupils were matched according to their self-views (e.g., all the pupils
who saw themselves as equally smart or equally hardworking), their
reputation still explained a significant amount of their differences
in competence. When, on the other hand, pupils were matched by
reputation (i.e., all the pupils who were seen by their classmates as
equally smart, hardworking, etc.), character was unrelated to their
actual competence. The implications of our study are twofold: First,
if what you think about yourself isn't shared by others, it probably
isn't true; second, even when you don't agree with others' views of
you, they probably are true.

And yet we tend to believe that our self-views are more accurate
than everybody else's views of us. Why? One of the reasons is that
doing so gives us a sense of control. Indeed, most of us operate under the illusion that our lives are totally unpredictable whereas other
people's lives are highly predictable. We even apply this asymmetric
logic to our judgments of our own and others' behavior, so we end
up adopting double standards: Others' behavior is usually attributed
to their nature (e.g., "they are stupid," "they are boring," "they are
disorganized"), but our own behavior is usually attributed to unpredictable external circumstances (e.g., "the train was late," "I got stuck
in a traffic jam," "it was his fault"), unless it is positive—in which
case we take credit by attributing that behavior to our ability or talents. The basis for this double standard is the assumption that we
are much more complex than others; that while others are prisoners
of their own nature, we are free to choose from a wide range of potential behaviors in any given situation. Others' character may be
destiny, but our own character is based on free will—or so we think.

Princeton psychologists Emily Pronin and Matthew Kugler have likened this "free will bias" to other self-serving biases. In a series of recent studies, they found that people tend to view their past and future as more unpredictable than their peers', that relative to others, their lives could have taken many more possible paths, and that their own lives—but not others'—are guided primarily by intentions and goals.[2] In one of their studies, Pronin and Kugler asked college students to estimate the probability that certain post-graduation events would occur for themselves and their roommates. Events included both positive (e.g., an exciting job, a nice apartment, falling in love) and negative (e.g., a boring job, a crappy apartment, being heartbroken) outcomes. As the researchers expected, students believed that fewer eventualities were possible for their classmates than themselves, even though that also implied that fewer negative outcomes were likely to occur for their classmates than themselves.

The free will illusion therefore eclipses other optimistic biases: Being better than others is less desirable than being freer than others, even when freedom brings more hardship. For example, study participants thought that the combined probability of having a nice or crappy apartment after graduating was 68 percent for themselves, but merely 32 percent for their roommates. They also estimated the combined probability of having great friends or not having enough friends to be 52 percent for themselves but only 28 percent for their roommates. As for the chances of having an exciting or boring job, the combined probability was 72 percent for themselves and 56 percent for their roommates. Across a wide range of life domains, then, participants thought that positive and negative outcomes were genuinely possible for themselves—such that their destiny was far from written—but that their roommates' destiny was much more constrained and written in stone. Obviously, their roommates will have some kind of outcome, just as the participants in the study will—so the results of this study demonstrate just how prevalent yet completely illogical this bias is.

It is worth noting, as well, that others' views of us do not need to be accurate in order to affect us. Robert Rosenthal and Lenore Jacobson conducted a now-famous experiment that involved providing elementary school teachers with the IQ scores of their pupils—but the information was made up. Knowledge of the pupils' alleged intelligence influenced the teachers' attitudes and behavior toward the pupils such that after inspecting the children's fake IQ scores, they started treating the purportedly smart students as if they were smart and the supposedly dim students as if they were dim. With time, teachers' false beliefs about their pupils' competence translated into actual performance increases (in the case of "smart" students) or decreases (in the case of "dim" students), an effect known as "self-fulfilling prophecy": A prediction about the future becomes true even though it is false at the time it is stated. Rosenthal and Jacobson called this the Pygmalion effect, after the mythical Greek sculptor who created a statue of a beautiful woman that then came to life to become his lover. Many Pygmalion effects, even in work rather than educational settings, have been reported since Rosenthal and Jacobson's original study.[3]

It is plausible to suggest that the self-fulfilling effects that others' perceptions of us have on us—especially when those others are in a position of power—are to blame for the achievement gap in domains where actual competence differences are nonexistent. For example, although there are no documented gender differences in IQ, many people, especially men, believe that men are smarter than women. As the Pygmalion effect demonstrates, if people assume that men are smarter than women, they will also start treating men as if they are smarter than women, which in turn causes achievement differences between men and women. In order to investigate this, my colleague Adrian Furnham and I have conducted many studies into others' estimates of people's competence. All of our studies show the same gender difference in others' estimates, with not just men but also women systematically rating males as more competent than females. The difference is especially pronounced when the raters are males—i.e., fathers see a bigger gap between their sons' and their daughters' competence than mothers do; sons reciprocate this by seeing the gap between their fathers' and mothers' intelligence as bigger than daughters do. Although this pattern is more pronounced in some countries than in others—"masculine" societies such as Turkey, Argentina, and Japan assume greater male superiority in competence than more "feminine" societies such as Denmark, Finland, and Sweden—it is found more or less everywhere. And remember, the sex differences in actual competence are *zero*, or even a small advantage for women over men (for example, in many developed or industrialized countries, such as the United States, women now outperform men in college). Indeed, more women than men attend college, and their grades are consistently higher.[4]

Likewise, despite ample evidence that men have no better leadership skills than women do, there is a disproportionately low number of women in management compared to men. For instance, there are only fourteen female CEOs among the top five hundred companies in the world. How can this happen if there are no actual sex differences in leadership competence? Because others' views of us (in this case women) need not be accurate in order to affect our (women's) lives.[5] When it comes to leadership, the majority of people who are in charge (men) see leadership as a masculine role. In a comprehensive review of scientific studies into people's conceptions of leadership, psychologist Anne Koenig, of the University of California, San Diego, reports conclusive evidence for the preponderance of sexist stereotypes about leaders and managers favoring men. She concludes that since society believes men make better leaders, then the definition of what it is to be a leader takes on masculine qualities. As such, it becomes much easier for men to become leaders and much harder for women to break into these roles. So then: "Given the strongly masculine cultural stereotype of leadership, these challenges are likely to continue for some time to come."[6]

Unsurprisingly, a survey of 705 senior female leaders (vice presidents or higher in Fortune 1000 companies) showed that 72 percent see "stereotypes about women's roles and abilities" as a huge barrier to career advancement.[7] And yet, research evidence suggests that women are more, not less, competent leaders than men are. For example, female leaders tend to care more about their subordinates and inspire them more; they are also less likely to take dangerous risks or to be corrupt. Clearly, then, more female leaders would be beneficial to both organizations and society.

Henry Ford famously stated that whether you feel that you can do it or not, you are right—implying that your confidence has self-fulfilling effects on your competence. The statement would be more accurate if it read "whether *others* feel that you can do it or not, they are usually right," especially when others know you well or when they have the power to decide your future.

Others Value Humility, Not Confidence

Against the backdrop of popular tips highlighting the social benefits of confidence, a wealth of research evidence indicates that, ultimately, we all value competence over confidence. In fact, when one subtracts competence from confidence, the remaining confidence—or confidence surplus—is perceived by others as undesirable. Conversely, when people appear to be more competent than they give themselves credit for, they are liked much more. Randall Colvin's studies on inflated self-views showed that when people's self-evaluations are more positive than others' evaluations of them, they have poorer and fewer relationships compared with people whose self-views align with others' views of them. In addition, reams of psychological studies show that being perceived as modest is associated with a wide range of positive outcomes. The message is clear: People do not value confidence unless it is accompanied by competence—and even when it is, they prefer to see as little confidence surplus as possible.

A team of psychologists from the University of Arizona, led by Dr. Wilhelmina Wosinska, conducted a study in which they provided participants with hypothetical scenarios describing successful colleagues (males and females) who reacted to a promotion with different degrees of modesty. Let's consider one such scenario, in which an employee who has worked with your company for five years has been shown to be the most productive in the past three months. You congratulate her in front of your colleagues, and tell her she must be very proud of herself. Having been presented with this scenario, each participant was faced with one of three potential reactions from the employee:

"Thanks, I am. I just knew I would win." (low modesty)
"Thanks, I heard about it unofficially this morning." (intermediate modesty)
"Thanks, but I think it was mostly luck." (high modesty)[8]

Participants then indicated how much support they would provide the candidate if they were that person's colleague or manager (e.g., publicize her achievements, put her up for a new promotion, give her more responsibilities, ask her to take on a leadership role). These ratings were aggregated into an overall likability score, which enabled Dr. Wosinska's team to compare the popularity of each level of modesty separately for male and female raters (the study participants) and targets (the imaginary characters in the scenarios).

I'm pretty sure you have already worked out that the low-modesty option was the least popular of the three. Indeed, whether participants were male or female, they tended to prefer the modest characters. When the characters were male, moderate modesty was preferred to high and low modesty, whereas for female characters high modesty was the favorite option.[9] The implications of this study are clear: Even if you are competent, modesty pays off and showing off doesn't. As Dr. Wosinska and colleagues concluded: "Unobtrusively doing great work (modesty) is not likely to threaten the self-esteem of co-workers. However, bringing attention to one's work (boasting) is likely to inspire resentment from co-workers."[10]

The advantages of modesty have also been highlighted by studies examining its real-world rather than hypothetical manifestations. Jim Collins, a leading authority on management, has spent more than thirty years investigating why certain organizations are more successful than others, and, especially, what the features of super successful businesses are.[11] His conclusion? Humble leadership. Indeed, Dr. Collins found that companies led by modest managers systematically outperformed their competitors, implying that the ideal leader is the exact opposite of the celebrity-style corporate managers typically portrayed in the media. Dr. Collins's conclusion is based on four well-documented facts: First, modest leaders stay in an organization for much longer than arrogant leaders. Second, companies led by humble managers tend to be the dominant player in their sectors. Third, these companies continue to perform well even after their leaders leave—because humble leaders care more about the organization and its employees than about themselves and therefore ensure a healthy succession is in place before they depart. Fourth, humble leaders are unlikely to be found cheating or involved in scandals. Cases of corruption, insider trading, extramarital affairs, and bullying are all associated with overconfident and arrogant managers. You need only open the newspaper for examples.

So what does all this mean? Competence is always better when coupled with less rather than more confidence. It is also clear that people are more interested in our competence than our confidence, and that they will generally like us more if we have lower rather than higher confidence. This is true regardless of *their* competence levels, but particularly when they have low competence. Note that all this holds true in our individualistic, narcissistic, and self-deluded Western world, where most of the research has been carried out. When you travel east or to any collectivistic society, modesty and competence are valued even more, to the point of self-censoring displays of hubris and embracing humility much more than we do in the West. But even in our self-obsessed culture, confidence is hardly an asset to seduce, impress, or intimidate others. Rather, humility, especially in the face of high competence, is what's valued.

Everyone's a Psychologist

If there is one thing people value more than modesty and competence, it's predictability. As we've seen, we like to think that other people are predictable (while we are *un*predictable). Indeed, one of the most consistent findings in modern psychology is that people have an intense need to work out what others will do next. This strong desire to predict others' behavior is what drives us to speculate about human nature—why is it that people do what they do and not something else? When you are a psychologist, the first question people ask when they find out what you do is whether you can read their mind. In reality, psychologists are no different from anyone else: Every person in this world is trying to work out what other people are thinking in order to predict what they will do next—even kids.

From the age of two, children begin to understand the goals and intentions of adults. By the age of five, they start realizing that others' beliefs may be false (that people may be wrong or mistaken in their thoughts). By the time we reach adulthood, we are 100 percent reliant on our interpretations of others' behaviors in our social interactions. We do this via a simple three-step process:

> *Step 1:* We observe a behavior that interests us—e.g., someone is looking at us.
> *Step 2:* We assess the person's motives—e.g., friendly, unfriendly, curious, neutral.
> *Step 3:* We attribute those motives to a cause—i.e., the person or the situation.

On the one hand, without making judgments about other people's intentions, there would be no prejudice or discrimination, which results from our assumption that a person's behavior is the result of his or her membership in certain groups (e.g., ethnicity, nationality, gender, sexual orientation). There would also be no fights, which result from the assumption that other people want to harm us or threaten our interests. And yet we can't function without interpreting people's behavior in one way or another. Without making judgments, we would have no:

- legal system (intention determines whether someone is guilty or not)
- close relationships (intention helps us understand whether people like us)
- business transactions (intention tells us what other people want from us)[12]

Consider the following scenario:

Have you ever sat on the bus or train facing other passengers? Even when the seats are laid out in such a way, etiquette tends to dictate that we should not gaze at other people for more than a few seconds at most, especially after they look back at us—usually a subtle request that we stop staring at them. Did you ever sit facing someone who just kept staring and staring at you? Anywhere in the world, that behavior would qualify as unusual. So, what do you do in this situation?

As per the three-step sequence, observing the person's behavior would be the first step (you notice that he keeps looking at you). The second step is trying to work out *why* he is looking at you (assessing his motive). Is he just curious; is he trying to work out whether he knows you from somewhere; is his motive friendly or unfriendly? Of particular importance here is your interpretation of the person's level of friendliness. If he seems unfriendly, you will infer a threat; if he seems friendly, you may interpret the situation as appealing, albeit still unusual. The final step is more important still. Attributing the person's intention to the situation implies that he does not normally stare at other passengers, which in turn implies that his behavior is somehow caused by you (e.g., the way you look or behave). On the other hand, attributing his intention to his personality or character would imply that his behavior has little to do with you (e.g., he is generally rude, curious, or both)—this is the most common interpretation, because it eliminates the possibility that there's something wrong with you. But how do people interpret behaviors when they are mere observers rather than also involved in the situation?

A reliable way to assess people's attributions of others' behaviors is the so-called "silent interview" method. This technique involves showing participants a mute video of a person behaving nervously during an interview. In one condition, participants are told that the interviewers are asking the candidate very tough questions. In another condition, participants are told that the interviewers are asking fairly friendly questions. Participants in each condition are then asked to describe the interviewee's personality. When participants are told that the questions are easy, they perceive the candidate's personality as much more anxious than when they are told that the interview involves tough questions. In both conditions, though, participants end up making strong inferences about the candidate's character by comparing the observed behavior with the behavior they would normally expect of someone—mostly themselves—in similar situations. It is noteworthy that even when the situation (i.e., a harsh interview) is strong enough to suspend any judgment about the interviewee's character, observers assume that the interviewee is usually calm, ignoring the possibility that typically anxious people may also react nervously to a tough or embarrassing interview (in fact, they are much more likely to do so than calm people are).

The moral of the story? People will always make assumptions about you and make attributions about your behavior, to the point of making up a theory about who you are and why you do what you do. We all behave like amateur psychologists, trying to work out what other people want, think, and feel in order to forecast what they will do next. Your personality concerns not just yourself, but everybody else, and its public face is a hundred times more consequential than your private self. More on this next.

Do Others Know What We Are Like? Do We?

How accurate are others' judgments of us? It is important to understand whether our observers' perceptions are valid, but how? What sort of benchmark can we use to test their validity? An obvious answer would be "our own perceptions," but given that most people are biased, how would we know whether we are right or wrong? That is, in the event of a discrepancy between others' views of us and our self-views, it would be hard to decide who's got it right. On the other hand, different people may perceive us in different ways, which begs the question of whose views of us we should consider in the first place. Luckily, scientific studies have addressed these issues.

Connelly and Ones analyzed the combined data from hundreds of studies (totaling more than forty thousand participants) on the relationship between people's self-perceptions and others' perceptions of them.[13] Their results suggest that there is some overlap between how others evaluate us and how we evaluate ourselves, but that there are more differences than similarities between these evaluations. Connelly and Ones also found that our self-views are more similar to certain people's views of us. Depending on who is evaluating us, there will be smaller or bigger discrepancies between their judgments of us and our self-views, which makes intuitive sense. For example, family members, friends, and long-term romantic partners see us in a way that closely resembles our own views of ourselves, but colleagues, occasional coworkers, and strangers often don't.

On the other hand, the similarity between our self-views and other people's views of us also seems to depend on the specific aspect of our character that is evaluated. For instance, others perceive our sociability and ambition similarly to how we perceive them ourselves, but when it comes to inferring our modesty, confidence, and especially our intellect, our self-views are much more discrepant from other people's views of us. This has been explained in terms of the "internal" or less observable nature of the more discrepant elements of our character. In contrast, sociability and ambition are more "external" (sociable people talk and laugh a lot; ambitious people are energetic and pushy) and hence more observable in nature. Does that imply that the "true" measure of our character is always our self-view, and that we should use our self-evaluations to validate other people's judgments of us?

Not really. Connelly and Ones examined the degree to which different observers agree in their evaluations of the same person (and remember, their findings are based on hundreds of independent scientific studies involving thousands of participants). As it turns out, even when others' impressions of us are quite different from our self-impressions, their views tend to be in agreement with each other. In other words, although we may see ourselves differently than other people see us, other people tend to have more or less the same picture of us, especially within the same category of closeness. Thus strangers tend to make the same judgments of an unknown person, coworkers make the same independent evaluations of their colleague, and different friends are in agreement about how they view their common friend.[14] What this suggests is that when our self-views differ substantially from the judgments other people make about us, it would make more sense to regard *their* views as accurate and ours as inaccurate, because, whatever they see, they are seeing the same thing. If we are the only ones seeing ourselves the way we do and everybody else sees us in the same way, how can we claim that they are wrong and we are right?

As a quote by Thomas Paine wisely suggests, our reputation is whatever other people think of us—whether we agree with them or not. In order to find out about our character we may need to ask God, the angels, or whatever divine power you believe in—Google, maybe? If you find this counterintuitive, perhaps that's because you frequently hear people say that you should not pay attention to what others think of you—this message is part of the ethos of the Kim Kardashian era in which we live. It promotes a *light* version of counterconformity based on a "be yourself, love yourself, and ignore what others think of you" philosophy, while simultaneously turning its adherents into mass-market consumers (and products). There is, in actuality, nothing new about our resistance to caring about our reputations. Over a century ago, the eminent American sociologist Charles Horton Cooley noted: "Many people scarcely know that they care what others think of them, and will deny, perhaps with indignation, that such care is an important factor in what they are or do."[15] It appears we haven't changed that much.

Why You Should Care About Others' Perceptions of You

Not only should you care about what others think of you; it's actually the only way you can have a coherent view of yourself in the first place. Others' perceptions of us may take into account how we see ourselves, but they are based mainly on what we do and not on what we think. It is easy to miss this point, not least because we spend a great deal of time thinking about ourselves—much more than others do anyway. However, people are interested in our actions rather than our beliefs. As the saying goes, "Your beliefs don't make you a better person; your behavior does." Pay attention to how you behave and, especially, what others make of your behavior, and you will have a very good sense of who you are. Fail to pay attention and you will end up having a very peculiar view of yourself—one that nobody else shares. If you want to avoid being self-centered, just be *other*-centered instead (it would be a considerable upgrade).

The idea that we should ignore other people's opinions of us is appealing, but silly. Why is it appealing? Because it is packaged as a passport to freedom and success. How so? By conveying the illusion that if we stop caring about what others think of us we will (a) relieve ourselves of the pressures of society and be free, and (b) achieve fame and status. Why is this silly? Because attaining fame and status is the exact opposite of freeing yourself from society, so the two alleged reasons for not caring about what other people think of us are mutually exclusive. Nobody achieves fame or status by ignoring others; everybody does so by precisely the opposite means—paying a great deal of attention to others and caring as much as possible about what they think. Throughout my career, I have coached many senior executives who had problems dealing with their colleagues, bosses, or subordinates. Without exception, the only people who managed to overcome their problems were those who understood that it was important, if not essential, to consider how they were perceived by others. And without exception, those who did not ended up derailing or downgrading to lower positions.

In line, ignoring other people's views of us will almost certainly eliminate the possibility of attaining fame or status, but would it "set us free"? No; in fact, it's essential that we are aware of what others think and are able to interpret their thoughts. Without the opportunity to pay attention to others' thoughts, we don't establish normal developmental processes, such as language acquisition (think, for example, of the extreme cases of children who were raised by wolves or chimps and passed the first years of their lives without human contact). Consider when children first learn to speak: They start by repeating the sounds (words) they hear, they connect those sounds with things, and then they use their limited vocabulary to ask questions about other things until more words replace the actual things in their minds. Crucially, the meaning always comes from other people. Therefore, if you cannot grasp what others think, you cannot grasp much at all. Children with developmental problems that impair their ability to understand others face this difficulty throughout their lives. The most notable example of this is autism, a spectral developmental disorder in which even those on the far end of the spectrum tend to lack interest in others and to be mentally isolated from the social world.

Many psychological studies, for example those conducted by Dr. Jennifer Beer and colleagues, have linked varying levels of deficits in perceiving and displaying self-conscious emotions to damage in a specific region of the brain, the orbitofrontal cortex, which rests behind the eyes and is responsible for regulating social interactions. In a series of experiments, Dr. Beer's team compared how participants with orbitofrontal lesions performed on self-disclosure tasks vis-à-vis healthy participants. For instance, one of the tasks required participants to talk about past situations in which they had felt embarrassed or guilty. Whereas healthy participants disclosed events that were generic, vague, and unrevealing (e.g., "I felt guilty when I hurt my friend's feelings" or "I felt embarrassment when I didn't understand a joke"), participants with orbitofrontal damage disclosed specific, personal, and inappropriate events (e.g., "I felt guilty when I cheated on my wife" or "I felt embarrassed when I was discovered having sex in the dressing room of a store"). Furthermore, when participants were asked to describe the emotions they felt when disclosing these events, those who had orbitofrontal lesions expressed no regret or embarrassment at telling these stories. In the real world, individuals' lack of awareness of how they are perceived by others just serves to marginalize them.

So rather than offering freedom or stardom, not seeing what others think of you will just detach you from the social world, which is the only world humans inhabit. There are, indeed, many reasons to argue that our capacity to infer other people's thoughts and emotions is what makes us quintessentially different from other species. Charles Cooley used the "looking glass" metaphor to describe the role of others in shaping our identity. As he noted, we view ourselves according to how we imagine other people view us. Our character is *reflected* in others, and our ability to see that reflection is what enables us to be aware of ourselves as individuals in society. When our confidence is higher than our competence, the reflection we see is too favorable; when our confidence is lower than our competence, the reflection we see is too unflattering. In other words, if we have notably low or high self-esteem, we have an inaccurate depiction of how others actually see us, which in turn will affect our social interactions. In line, the eminent philosopher George H. Mead argued that "the individual mind can exist only in relation to other minds with shared meanings."[16] More recently, renowned psychologist Roy Baumeister argued that humans evolved to experience the need for close bonds with others—what he terms "belongingness"—and that our self-esteem has evolved for two main reasons, namely to alert us to behaviors that disrupt social relations and to trigger behaviors that promote close social relations. For instance, if someone has low self-esteem because he is unhappy about his weight, the low self-esteem would drive him to change in order to avoid being rejected by others. If someone is feeling down because she lost her job or failed a college exam, low self-esteem levels would signal to her that she risks losing approval from others and may be jeopardizing relationships, and so on. Thus, even our deepest and innermost emotions are linked to and shaped by other people, and these emotions play a key role in helping us attain, nurture, and restore healthy relationships with others.

Over the past three decades psychologists have carried out hundreds of scientific studies into the nature of what they refer to as "self-conscious emotions"—shame, pride, guilt, embarrassment, etc. These emotions are different from basic emotions such as joy, anger, sadness, and disgust in that they are reactions to others' perceptions of us. As Mark Leary, a leading expert in the field, noted: "Self-conscious emotions fundamentally involve drawing inferences about other people's evaluations rather than simply comparing one's behavior to personal self-representations."[17] Self-conscious emotions tend to develop with age, which is why they are not found in young children. You may have noticed, for instance, that children are rarely embarrassed or ashamed in situations in which the typical adult would be. But as we grow older, we become increasingly sensitive to what others think of us, such that self-conscious emotions develop and acquire growing importance in adulthood, better enabling us to function in society. In line, adult emotions originate from our perceptions of our reputation. As Dr. Beer and her colleagues at the University of California, Berkeley, explain, these self-conscious emotions are strongly linked to how we think other people see us, rather than how we actually view ourselves.

For example, Dr. Beer's team found that most individuals tend to be embarrassed when they think that others evaluate them negatively, even when they are aware that their actual evaluations are not really that negative. By the same token, others' evaluations can make us feel ashamed or guilty even when we know that we did not do anything wrong. As the authors argued, "People experience self-conscious emotions not because of how they evaluate themselves but rather because of how they think they are being evaluated or might be evaluated by others."[18]

So, in order to have an accurate view of yourself, it is absolutely essential that you pay attention to others' views of you, contrary to what so many self-help gurus and confidence blogs prescribe. Failing to consider others' views will neither set you free nor make you successful; rather, it will create an inaccurate and deluded self-view and disrupt your relationships with others. Nietzsche was right when he pointed out that it is easier to cope with a bad conscience than a bad reputation. Having a bad conscience is a sign that you care about others; having a bad reputation is a sign that you don't.

Self-Knowledge Matters More Than Self-Belief

One of the features of expertise is the ability to recognize how limited our knowledge is. This is why many of the greatest minds this world has seen have repeatedly highlighted the negative effects of confidence on competence. Socrates, the father of Western philosophy, famously noted that the only thing he knew was that he didn't know anything at all, and others shared this way of looking at themselves. Many centuries later, Voltaire, the French philosopher and poet, and one of the leading intellectual figures of the Enlightenment, echoed Socrates's remark by noting that as he read more, he became more aware and more certain that really he did not know anything. Along those lines, Charles Darwin, one of the most influential scientists in history and the genius behind evolutionary theory, observed that confidence is more often caused by ignorance than by knowledge. And the list goes on. Shouldn't we heed the warnings of the most brilliant intellects of all time?

More recently, psychological research has indicated that the least competent people are the most likely to be overconfident, because they lack the ability to understand just how incompetent they are. This effect has been found in virtually every domain of competence: sense of humor, good taste, creativity, intelligence, and a wide range of physical skills. For instance, the less funny people are, the more they overrate their sense of humor; the less taste they have, the better taste they think they have; and the dimmer they are, the more they overrate their intelligence. In short, incompetence leads to both poor performance and the inability to realize that one is incompetent.

When I first started teaching, I thought I could just stand in front of the class and freestyle my lecture. I was so confident in my ability to *edutain* (educate + entertain) that I never even bothered preparing. Although the classes were fun, the best students quickly worried about the lack of structure and content. They looked at the course syllabus and realized that I was not covering most of the topics, and that they would have to cover everything by themselves through independent studying. On the other hand, the less ambitious students thought the class was great, because they assumed that there was nothing to be learned or studied. I was so pleased with myself that I dismissed any negative feedback from the students and instead focused on the positive comments: "Finally someone decided to make the lectures entertaining," "At last one lecturer who encourages a lot of interaction and discussion." These may have been true, but at the same time I was failing to teach my students what they were meant to learn as part of the course.

When, a few years later, I started paying attention to students' negative evaluations (because they became more and more common), I was slightly demoralized at first. My teaching confidence dropped, which also made me question my overall competence for academia. However, that unpleasant realization helped me take the first crucial steps toward improving my teaching: making sure students had all the key readings, planning my lectures carefully, etc. Although my teaching confidence has never reached the level it did at the beginning of my academic career, students' feedback has since improved substantially, because my teaching competence improved. The point I am trying to make is that high confidence can be a curse because it can stop you from improving. If you are really satisfied with your performance you will tend to ignore negative feedback, distorting reality in your favor. By the same token, lower confidence can be a blessing if it helps you pinpoint your weaknesses and motivates you to improve. So, when competence is low, confidence (self-belief) is often high. But if you start to take on board others' assessments of you (ratings of your competence), your self-knowledge will increase and your self-belief can become more in line with reality.

Psychological research shows that higher confidence increases people's tendency to dismiss or disqualify the sources of negative feedback, as well as to praise those who think favorably of them.[19] Try telling people who are very pleased with themselves that they are not good at something and they will either think you are joking or confront you. People with an optimistic mind-set and higher generic self-confidence are especially likely to distort reality in their favor after receiving negative feedback, something called "compensatory self-inflation."[20] The distorting effects of confidence have been visualized in our brains, as brain-scanning studies identified specific brain regions responsible for representing and processing feedback from others. Indeed, recent studies show that the brains of confident and unconfident people differ in their responses to praise and criticism from others.[21]

Dr. Sharot and her fellow neuroscientists at UCL have also identified specific brain areas and mechanisms underlying optimistic biases in particular.[22] It seems that the brains of optimists (i.e., those whose perspectives show a more positive view than may be warranted) are much more able (or willing) to ignore evidence of negative events, such that they fail to send a chemical signal to alert our consciousness of the fact that things may not be looking good. Just like the ostrich that buries its head under the sand to avoid danger, the self-delusional brains of confident people are naturally prewired to "defend" themselves from threats by ignoring them, which is of course ultimately ineffective. Accordingly, higher confidence threatens self-knowledge because it limits people's willingness to understand how others truly see them, which precludes their understanding of who they are.

Another explanation for the fact that the least competent people are the most likely to be overconfident is that people are generally too polite to provide them with negative feedback about their incompetence, which would help them improve. Instead, we act as if they are competent, which only serves to confirm their inflated self-views. Generally speaking, as adults we tend to act with the fake politeness we demand from young children when we tell them that if they don't have anything nice to say they should just remain quiet.

The preponderance of polite fake feedback explains the popularity of talent-based reality TV shows such as *American Idol*, which expose a huge gap between participants' confidence and their competence.[23] These contestants perform with the confidence of a maven, but often deliver a dismal performance, especially in the initial rounds. This is what makes the audition episodes of *American Idol* so amusing: Some of the contestants have so little talent that it is impossible not to give them negative feedback—even the nicest judges are excused for being brutally honest with them. The fact that reality TV sometimes provides a more honest version of reality than the one we find in the real world can go a long way toward explaining the popularity of such shows: Viewers get to see overconfident but undercompetent hopefuls receive a sharp dose of reality, which in day-to-day settings is a rare occurrence. In real life, we devote way too much time to providing positive feedback to those who don't deserve it, which contributes to inflating their confidence (yet not their competence). This is akin to what the judges of another, similar talent-based reality TV show, *The Voice*, do with contestants: Although most of them are as talentless as *American Idol*'s, the judges are as hypocritical (or polite) as most people in the real world are; this may explain the lower ratings of this show vis-à-vis *American Idol*.

Using It:

- Although confidence is often very different from competence, others will look to your outward displays of confidence in order to assess your competence, so it is to your advantage to display confidence even if you don't feel it, as it will make it harder for others to spot your weaknesses. However, beware of displaying too much confidence if you are unable to back it up—others don't like it when confidence is not backed up by competence. Conversely, they will like you more if you are more competent than you claim, and if you are modest about your achievements.

- Competence needs to be boosted in a way that others will notice; otherwise it will make no difference in how they see you.

- Through self-fulfilling prophecies, what others believe about our competence *does* affect us.

- Reputation (how others see you) is more accurate than your self-view as a representation of how competent you are (i.e., others can gauge your competence levels more accurately than you can).

- Having an accurate perception of your reputation will help you function well in society and know how to respond to others, avoiding the possibility of marginalizing yourself through a lack of awareness about how you are perceived.

- High confidence often masks low competence, which can be a curse, as it stops you from working to improve. Low confidence helps you see your weaknesses and motivates you to overcome them. It's better to have realistic self-knowledge than distorted self-belief, so that you can know what you need to work on to get better.

4

A Successful Career

There are two rules to success in life: 1. Don't tell people
everything you know.   —Unknown

What Top Performers Do Better

In this chapter, I'll expose some common pieces of career wisdom
as myth: most notably, that professional success does not come
simply as a result of high confidence or self-belief; neither does it
depend on innate talent. By the end of the chapter you should have
a realistic understanding of what top performers actually do to accomplish big things, providing you with the necessary insight to
boost your own career success. As you may have already guessed,
the easiest way to do this is to boost your competence.

Debunking Career Myths
(Confidence, Talent, and Arrogance)

Here's a simple quiz for you. Think about someone who is hugely
successful—anyone, famous or not. Now try to work out whether

the person is low or high on the following three traits: confidence, talent, and arrogance. My guess is that you rated that person high on confidence. In fact, if I asked you to think about someone who is very successful but lacks confidence, you would probably need to think for a long time—but only because we are less likely to remember successful people when they are humble, kind, and low-key. I would also guess that you rated the person high on talent, unless you have chosen someone you resent for being too rich or more successful than you think he or she deserves to be. As for arrogance, unless you picked someone you really like (which would bias your judgment), you probably rated that person as arrogant rather than modest.

I have spent much of the past two decades trying to understand why some people are more successful than others, a quest that has led me to read roughly one thousand books, conduct more than fifty experiments, interview hundreds of experts, and collaborate with many of the leading authorities in the field. I think about this question all the time. All in all, I have examined data for at least one million individuals across different fields of competence—business, college, arts, sports, and even criminal activities—talking to them, studying their biographies, and testing them with the best available methods and tools. Many of these studies enabled me to follow up with people for several years. I have also coached thousands of people to help them become more successful in their careers.

My conclusion?

Whatever people do, their career success always depends on the same three factors, and confidence is *not* one of them. It probably won't surprise you by now to know that, more often than not, lower confidence is more advantageous than higher confidence. But before we examine the three things top performers have in common, let me debunk some of the common myths about the key determinants of career success.

Myth 1: You Can Be Anything You Want
If You Believe in Yourself

Let's get this straight: Successful people tend to be more confident, but only because they are usually more aware of their competence. In reality, successful people do not differ much in their confidence levels from their less successful peers. Consider the following fact: The correlation between career success and any measure of career confidence is .30 at most, which suggests that if we measured someone's confidence in order to estimate how successful he may be, we would be only 15 percent more accurate than if we just guessed. And that is the largest correlation reported by any credible independent study. Moreover, the modest overlap between career confidence and competence is mostly accounted for by the effects of competence on confidence rather than vice versa. In other words, career success boosts career (and generic) confidence, but no form of confidence has been found to have concrete, observable, or meaningful positive effects on career competence.

One of the greatest thinkers this world has ever seen, the Scottish philosopher David Hume, noted in the eighteenth century what psychologists observed only three hundred years later, namely that it is not possible for us to directly observe any form of cause and effect in the real world. All we can do is observe *covariations*: When X happens so does Y; when someone is successful, she is confident, etc. The key covariation regarding the role of confidence in career success (and one of the reasons you probably had for buying this book) is that "confident people seem more successful"; ergo, you may be inclined to think, "If I sort out my confidence problems, I will be more successful in my career"—but you shouldn't. First, the confidence–career success correlation is small—many successful people are not that confident, and there are even more unsuccessful people who are *very* confident (I am sure you can think of examples). Second, when people are both successful and confident, their confidence is more often a product of their success than vice versa. And yet, unless you live in total isolation from the rest of the world, you have probably been brainwashed into believing that high self-belief is the most important single cause of career success; that if you *think* you can do something, you most certainly will.

When scientific studies measure not just current levels of confidence and career success but also *previous* competence (e.g., talent, skill, or potential), the already small correlation between confidence and career success disappears. For example, one of our studies tested thousands of school pupils on initial competence (their school performance), subsequent career confidence, and later academic performance. The kids who were more confident at age nine tended to do a bit better in their studies at age twelve. However, when we took into account how they had performed *until* age nine, it became clear that the only reason for their higher confidence was their previous higher competence—that they had done well in the first place. The path is quite simple and intuitive: Kids who do well feel confident because they did well; kids who feel confident despite not having done well don't end up doing any better. Competence leads to confidence, but not vice versa.[1]

My team and I have replicated these findings with college students. In many studies involving thousands of universities from all over the world (literally; we looked at data from five continents), students who displayed higher levels of confidence tended to have better grades—but it was their *previous* grades that led to higher levels of confidence; confidence did not cause any competence gains. There was only one exception to this rule: males. Indeed, when we broke down the results by sex we noticed that although male students tended to display higher levels of confidence than did females, males' grades were generally not higher, but lower. Furthermore, analyzing the data for male students only, those who displayed higher levels of confidence were often performing *worse* academically than those who displayed lower confidence levels. This shows that male confidence is delusional, and that the more overconfident males are, the more incompetent they tend to be.

Looking at the combined data for both sexes, we found that males almost always exhibited more confidence than females did, despite the fact that they were being systematically outperformed by them. So what do these findings mean? Men are cocky and it doesn't pay off. Women are modest and it doesn't harm them. And that's not the end of the story: Women are less delusional than men when it comes to assessing their academic career potential, and that *does* pay off. In fact, in almost every country around the globe women's academic performance has been rising, often to the point of outperforming men (this is certainly the case in the United States), yet men remain more confident in their career success than women do.[2]

What about those beyond college? Good question. Psychological research is often based just on college students, who are hardly representative of the overall population, though one day they will hopefully become adults. As it turns out, when it comes to the relationship between confidence and adult career success (competence postcollege), the findings from our unrepresentative high school and college students are replicated almost perfectly with grown-ups. And as with students, the modest positive association found between adult confidence and career success (the .30 correlation) is *not* indicative of the effects of confidence on career success; rather, it is indicative of the fact that more successful people tend to be more confident about their career success. In other words, being more talented makes you more competent, which in turn makes you more confident. Given that competent people tend to come across as confident, and that individuals who lack confidence tend to be aware of their incompetence, the gap between career confidence and competence is not always easily observable. Still, most confident people are not as competent as they think, and most competent people are confident only as a result of being competent, which they did not achieve by being confident.

Myth 2: Success Depends on Innate Talent

Another misconception about successful people is that they are innately talented. Unless you are talking about Pablo Picasso, Marie Curie, or Albert Einstein—the top .01 percent of performers in a field—it's safe to say that talent is overrated, especially innate talent. By "innate talent" I mean the exceptional skills or gifts with which one might be born. However, the only examples in which such innate talent can be seen are famous child prodigies. For instance, Wolfgang Amadeus Mozart (1756–1791) could memorize a major composition in less than half an hour by the age of four. He began composing at the age of six and when he was eight he composed his first full symphony. Pablo Picasso (1881–1973) allegedly made portraits of his sister when he was a baby, using egg yolks. At the age of fourteen, he was accepted to one of the most prestigious art academies in the country. *The Picador*, his first masterpiece, was produced when he was eight years old. Finally, Nadia Elena Comăneci (born 1961), the Romanian gymnast, became the first female gymnast to achieve a perfect score of 10 during an Olympic event, the Montreal 1976 Olympic Games, at the age of fifteen; she was awarded three gold medals. These examples illustrate the innate talent each was born with; its consequence is documented in the form of their career success at such young ages. However, aside from these incredibly rare examples, for at least 99 percent of the world's population, innate talent has very little relevance.

At best, we can have a predisposition to do things better than others do—a tendency to develop certain skills better than others can, or to devote more time, attention, and energy to certain activities. Take any two people and one of them will have more potential (for whatever you are interested in) than the other. However, potential means nothing unless it is harnessed. In fact, we would not even talk about potential unless someone decided to develop it a bit in the first place. For instance, when we say someone has talent for playing the piano, it is because that person has already devoted some time developing piano-playing skills; when we say someone has talent for singing, it is because the person has decided to practice and perform songs in the first place; and when we assess someone's potential for leadership (e.g., in politics, business, or sports), it is because that person is already in a position where his or her management skills are noticeable.

The common claim in the biographies of great leaders that their leadership skills were already evident on the playground or at the age of five is sheer fiction. Would you like your president to be five or eight years old? Can a twelve-year-old manage a business? Even Mark Zuckerberg is older than that, and there is little evidence that he can manage a business, which is why he has appointed someone experienced to do so.[3] Thus although certain convictions and aptitudes may be manifested early on in a person's life, expertise and talent develop with experience, as a consequence of hard work, dedication, and focus.

More important, think about all the talented people who are *not* successful in their careers. How many do you know? Can't think? Here's a simple exercise to help you work it out: Browse through your Facebook contacts and count the number of people in your network you consider talented. Then count the number of people you consider successful. My guess is that your list of friends includes fewer successful than talented people. I am also pretty sure that there will be little overlap between the two categories. Some of your contacts will be talented but not successful; others will be successful but not talented. And among those for whom you tick both boxes (people who are both successful and talented), how many do you think owe their success to their innate talents? Exactly.

Thousands of psychological studies have tracked early manifestations of individuals' talents (measured during their first five to ten years of life) into later stages of life. How do they affect school, college, and finally job performance? The results are compelling: The only innate skill that affects later career success is learning potential. In other words, among children, fast learners will tend to be more successful when they grow up. Let me repeat this slowly: That is the *only* innate skill or, if you prefer, element of talent that has any long-standing impact on an individual's subsequent career success. And upon closer inspection the robust scientific evidence suggests that the effects of innate learning potential are rather trivial.

The best longitudinal studies in this area measure not only talent at time one and career success at time two (for example, five years later), but a wide range of psychological traits and life events in between those two time intervals. This is what the best studies look like: They administer various measures of talent, such as valid IQ tests, when the kids are five to ten years old, measure their school performance a few years later, assess their college performance and educational achievements later, and track their entire employment history after that. The findings? No prizes for guessing. The kids who learned faster tended to be more successful in their careers, but only because they did better in school and college, and because they did better in training once they got the job.[4] There is therefore a domino- or snowball-style chain of events: Higher learning potential helps you do better in school, which then helps you do better in college, which then helps you do better when you are being trained for the job, which then helps you do better on the job. This logical transition from earlier skills to later expertise explains why faster learners have an advantage as kids, adolescents, and adults. And that's where the documented advantages of any innate skill end.

Myth 3: Arrogant People Are More Successful

Can you think of a CEO who isn't a bastard? Or a powerful corporate manager who really cares about others? Have you met many successful people who seemed modest? Do you really believe celebrities when they try to come across as nice, caring, or considerate in media interviews? No, no, no, and no, and many people agree with you. Still, you don't need to be arrogant in order to be successful—in fact, it actually helps if you are not. Luckily, there are not that many Donald Trumps in this world.

Real world data tells a very clear story:

- The most important attributes that successful corporate managers have are trustworthiness, kindness, and empathy. How do we know this? Because over the past fifty years there have been more than five hundred scientific studies assessing the profile of successful leaders across all types of industries and sectors and all over the world. The bottom line: Arrogant leaders are disliked by their bosses, their peers, and their subordinates, even in autocratic settings like the military.[5]

• The past ten years have shown that women tend to make better leaders than men. Why? Because they are generally more trustworthy, kind, and empathetic. True, there are fewer women than men in corporate senior leadership roles, but only because until recently (and still today in many parts of the world) women were not even allowed to aspire to top management jobs. Moreover, those who have the power to enable women to get those jobs (a.k.a. men) often operate under the stereotypical or prejudiced assumption that men are better leaders than women, partly because they don't realize that arrogance is a destructive leadership quality.[6]

• Although there are still many arrogant people in management (not only men), arrogance is neither necessary nor desirable to get to those positions, and it almost certainly guarantees failure once people get there, if they ever do. Gallup, the global consultancy that specializes in the assessment of employee engagement, reports that 60 to 70 percent of employees worldwide are either dissatisfied or seriously unhappy with their jobs, and that the single most important cause of this dissatisfaction is incompetent management. This data is based on thirty years of research and comprises seventeen million employees.[7] Indeed, when bosses are arrogant, their subordinates end up hating their jobs and quitting. As the saying goes, "People join organizations but quit their bosses." And when they don't quit, they don't perform to the best of their capabilities, engaging in counterproductive work behaviors (e.g., cheating, stealing, gossiping, or spending hours on Facebook).

Therefore, there should be far fewer arrogant people in charge than there currently are. For the sake of socioeconomic growth, political progress, and our sanity, we should work to prevent arrogant individuals from advancing in their careers at the peril of other people. The two reasons why arrogant people sometimes end up being successful is that they prioritize getting ahead at the expense of getting along—being ruthless, manipulative, exploitative, and bullish—and because their high confidence (arrogance) is often mistaken for competence.

On a slightly more positive note, in my career I have met, interviewed, studied, and coached hundreds of successful people from around the world and all sorts of jobs. Many of them were arrogant, yes, but the vast majority of arrogant people were not really successful, and the vast majority of really successful people were anything but arrogant. It's just sad that arrogance is something we often notice and remember people for—just think back to the prime example of Donald Trump: The very reason he stands out is that he is an exception (something that would normally not happen in the real world). If it were not for his obscene arrogance we might actually be allowed to forget who he is. Thankfully, though, arrogant people usually end up doing worse, whereas gentle, generous, and modest people end up doing better. So, whenever you see someone successful acting in an arrogant way, ask yourself if that person is truly competent, or if he is disguising his incompetence with his confidence. Sometimes, arrogance can be the most obvious disguise for a person's incompetence, and even mask his insecurities—why else would he need to bring others down in order to big himself up?

Three Things Top Performers Do Better

OK, so if career success isn't a function of self-belief, innate talent, or arrogance, what *are* the keys to this type of success? The answer is almost the exact opposite of what our three debunked myths imply. Indeed, modesty and kindness are much more useful than arrogance; a strong work ethic matters much more than innate talent; and confidence is only useful when coupled with competence.

Let's consider the principal driver of career success in developed economies: An individual's career success depends not on being employed, but on being *employable*. Jobs are temporary, but the ability to gain and maintain employment is a major lifelong career competence.[8] In the United States, only 65 percent of the potential workforce is employed,[9] and at least 40 percent of unemployed people have been jobless for a minimum of two years.[10] Although this is often blamed on the poor state of the economy, especially since the latest financial meltdown, there are two ongoing reasons for the poor employment prospects millions of people are facing today.

First, there is a generic mismatch between what various job markets demand and what potential employees can supply, resulting in a shortage of skills in some areas. This is the critical element in the "war for talent," in which employers compete fiercely for top-performing employees. In contrast, there is a clear surplus of skills in other areas: People who are out of work tend to have skills that are no longer sought after. Second, since the 1980s, businesses have stopped promising permanent jobs. For example, in 1983 the average U.S. male worker aged fifty-five to sixty-four had been with his employer for more than fifteen years, but this figure is now less than ten years. On average, U.S. workers remain at a job for less than four years. The dream of lifetime employment with a single organization has been replaced by the prospect of multiple career changes; the new psychological contract emphasizes "employability . . . work-centered adaptability that enhances individuals' ability to identify and seize career opportunities . . . employability is fundamental to maintain a career."[11] The message is clear: If you want to be successful in your career, you need to enhance your employability, but how?

Although there are hundreds of skills and millions of jobs, your employability depends on a fairly small set of criteria. In fact, the main criterion is always the same, namely whether you *seem* employable to your boss, client, or contractor. Employability, then, is an attribution someone makes about your likelihood to contribute positively to her business, or to help her attain her own commercial interests. To be employable means to be perceived as an attractive business partner or employee by a client or boss. So, why are some people perceived as more employable than others? The answer comes in the form of three things top performers do better.

#1: Display Competence

Top performers always come across as more competent or able. Of course, you may seem competent in certain domains but incompetent in others. However, what matters is how competent a potential employer or client thinks you are in relation to work-relevant tasks. The question here concerns your occupational expertise, your know-how, your reputation for solving problems related to the job in question. This is what people assess when they inspect your résumé, qualifications, or credentials. If you went to a good university or out-line a number of useful skills and accomplishments in your résumé (e.g., languages, computer skills, driver's license), employers will as-sume that you are competent in those domains. Of course, this may not be the case, because there are no perfect measures of an indi-vidual's performance until, well . . . they actually perform. Instead, the best employers can do is make informed, data-based predictions—taking into account your résumé, interview performance, test results, etc. Develop a strong résumé: Spend time on it and get feedback and opinions from other people on what they believe it says about you. Ultimately it is about being proactive in displaying your competence. Practice interviews, become informed, train in different software, and become an expert!

Whether you have worked hard enough to demonstrate compe-tence or not, you still need to ensure that you seem competent to others. Demonstrating competence is 10 percent of the achievement equation, namely your performance; the remaining 90 percent is your preparation. Assuming that you prepare as much as you possibly can, all you need is to ensure that you don't underperform too much. However, with proper preparation you can even get away with under-performance. For instance, people with high IQs will score high on IQ tests even if they are distracted when they take the test.[12] Addi-tionally, if a person has spent weeks studying the minutiae of a po-tential employer and learned all there is to know about how the company operates, even if on the day of his interview he is suddenly overcome with panic and fear, it will be evident he knows what he is talking about when asked questions relating to the company. His underperformance in the interview is likely to be forgotten because of his obvious level of preparation. The fact of the matter is, when you are very knowledgeable on a subject, it's not generally difficult to demonstrate your knowledge to others, even when nerves make you forget the odd fact. Your achievement depends on your performance, but your performance depends on your preparation, which, you'll remember, is negatively affected by confidence. Once you are competent at something, others will often notice it. However, if you lack competence, there are still occasions when you will be able to fool others (especially those not very good at judging people's competence) into believing that you are competent.

When you perform, it is useful to fake confidence because it will make you seem more competent to others. Failing to do so is like *not* exaggerating on your résumé—because most people will assume that you are exaggerating. Only people with undisputed expert credentials can afford not to brag. Moreover, true experts are able to demonstrate competence by faking *low* confidence or modesty. For instance, the Twitter bio of Malcolm Gladwell, one of the most successful nonfiction authors of our time, originally read, "Staff writer for *New Yorker Magazine*. I've also written some books," and now reads—even more modestly—"Curious journalist." If you want more examples, just tune in to the Academy Awards ceremony and listen to the various acceptance speeches: The most common denominator is the alleged humility of the winners, but that's only because they have won. In order to be "humble in victory," one first needs to be victorious—however, faking modesty is now so common among experts that it is often a good strategy for faking competence, a sort of double bluffing. So, here's my advice:

When you are competent, fake modesty.
When you are not, fake competence.
And if you cannot fake competence,
then try to fake confidence.

Faking modesty is a common presentational strategy in Britain, where people show off the most by pretending to lack competence or confidence. The standard way of displaying confidence or competence is to answer the question "How good are you at X?" by saying "Not too bad" or "OK, actually." It's a killer strategy because it will make others *add* rather than subtract 20 to 30 percent of competence to your claim. And here comes the best part: If you are naturally unconfident, you don't have to fake humility, because you will be perceived as modest anyway.

When you are used to seeing talentless people pretending to be competent, it is so refreshing to see someone who doesn't show off that you end up persuading yourself that he or she must be competent. More than once, I have been fooled (or fooled myself) into believing that some very quiet people were in fact competent but modest, when they were actually just clueless. Sadly, modest people may not get the credit they deserve, especially in situations when they are perceived as unenthusiastic, lazy, or incompetent, but this is only because narcissists exist in abundance. It is a real shame that there is so much admiration for those who overindulge in self-promotion. People who talk about themselves a lot and pretend to know everything about anything are often perceived as charming and competent, but merely because so many people are incapable of differentiating between confidence and competence. As Rob Kaiser, a well-known leadership consultant, once told me: "My biggest threat is the naïveté of my competitor's clients." This line could be applied to any domain of career success and life.

So, top performers display competence and tend to be modest about it. To emulate these people, starting with adequate preparation is key, as you have seen. Not only does this develop your competence; it will also override potential underperformances. Additionally, those at the top of their game appear to be extremely humble and modest about their competence. While this genuine modesty cannot be really achieved until you have been victorious in your pursuits, modesty is certainly something you can fake a little to help people perceive you as competent. However, and very important, society as a whole would benefit greatly by getting better at distinguishing between confidence and competence. This is because the talentless people who use bravado and overconfidence to get ahead would not be going anywhere.

#2: Work Hard

The second reason why people are deemed employable is that they are seen as hardworking, usually because they are. People often compensate for their relative lack of competence with hard work. In line, high-performing people just work much harder than their peers. Our research suggests that being smart increases the likelihood of being lazy, while realizing that you are not so smart motivates you to work harder to accomplish your goals.[13] In line, a series of now-seminal studies by Claudia Mueller and Carol Dweck demonstrated that children's assumptions about the nature of talent (intelligence) have important effects on their career success. In contrast to the widely held belief that praising the intelligence of children encourages motivation, these authors showed that it actually has more negative consequences regarding their motivation for achievement than praising *effort*. It was found that young children who had their intelligence praised placed more importance on their goals relating to performance than learning, in comparison with children who had their effort praised. These children (praised for intelligence) also tended to enjoy the tasks less, refusing to persist in them if they initially failed, and showed worse task performance than those who had their effort praised. Praising the effort and hard work of children also led them to believe their task performance could be improved.[14]

In his bestselling book *Outliers*,[15] Malcolm Gladwell argues, based on the work of Swedish psychologist Anders Ericsson,[16] that ten thousand hours of practice can turn you into a top performer in any field. The ten-thousand-hour rule is not the only factor determining people's success (there's also talent and opportunity), but it is uncommon to find exceptional achievers who have worked fewer hours at their craft. Let me save you from the calculations: If you work eight hours a day, seven days a week, it will take you almost three and a half years to accumulate the necessary working hours to become an expert, which tends to be the minimum time frame for completing a PhD program. The implications of the ten-thousand-hour rule are clear: It may be in your hands to be exceptional, but you will have to, if you'll pardon my language, work your ass off. Now, who do you think is more likely to double their efforts to attain their career goals—people who are confident about their performance or those who are not? Correct. Once again, confidence has inverse effects on competence.

Employers will sometimes be split over their decision to hire a candidate who is talented but potentially lazy or one who is less talented but seemingly hardworking and therefore a better potential performer. However, when two candidates appear equally competent, employers will always select the more driven individual, as she or he will end up outperforming the less driven candidate 85 percent of the time. Indeed, the best employees are rarely the most talented ones; rather, they are the ones who respond quickly, get stuff done, and produce exactly what is asked of them, if not more. As Bruce Tulgan notes in his clever essay on talent, a single truly great person on your team is worth numerous mediocre ones. [17]

Therefore, if you want to be successful in your career, you have to work hard, no matter how talented you are, and whatever your confidence. I really shouldn't be reminding you of this, but given the large number of people who believe that they can have a career by just showing up, I decided to dedicate an entire section to emphasizing how important a strong work ethic is. As Phillip Brown and Anthony Hesketh, the authors of *The Mismanagement of Talent*, argue, having an impressive résumé does not guarantee a motivated and driven attitude. Being proactive is a characteristic that is becoming increasingly sought after by employers, to the extent that it is shifting the traditional focus from capability. In the view of the authors, what sets leaders and top performing individuals apart from the rest is "that 'extra something' that comes from a deep hunger or drive for achievement and success."[18] Given that hunger and drive are extinguished with accomplishments, and that accomplishments breed confidence, it's best to use your lower confidence to stay hungry and driven.

3: Be Likable

The third key feature of top performers is that they are generally more likable. Indeed, people who are pleasant are more employable than unpleasant, dull, or difficult people.[19] So here's another piece of advice that sounds a lot more obvious than it actually is, at least given its low implementation rates: If you want a successful career, be kind to people, or at the very least, don't be a pain in the neck.

If you work for someone else, your promotion and career success are in the hands of your boss. In a just world, your boss would pay attention to your work contribution and value you for what you give to the organization. In the real world, managers are usually biased and hardly ever distinguish between employees' objective output and the degree to which they like or dislike them.[20] Thus, being liked by your boss will greatly affect your career success. Be nice to your manager and avoid confrontation; don't be a problem for him but, rather, someone whose company he enjoys. It will get you promoted faster than you think.

Managers will rarely admit this (they would be sued or fired), but between a boring employee who does a good job and a fun employee who does an average job, they would generally promote and retain the latter over the former. Next time your boss shows some favoritism for someone, remember that she is just like everyone else (including you), in that she finds some people more pleasant, rewarding, and fun than others. The only difference is she has decision-making power over your career. Note also that a bias toward likable employees will not necessarily have counterproductive effects for the organization—it is often the other way around. People who are rewarding to deal with impact positively on others: Their colleagues like having them around and so do their bosses, so they tend to exert a positive influence on staff morale and are important for maintaining good team spirit, which in turn causes businesses to perform better.

One problem with "sucking up" is that it is not always easy to implement, even when you accept the fact that it is extremely useful for your career. There are two main reasons for this. First, as Gallup's employee engagement data suggests,[21] most employees are managed ineptly, not least because they have pushy, bold, and truly intolerable bosses. This makes it extremely hard to be nice to them—you almost need to be a mercenary to do so. Second, we all (not just your boss) have a "dark side," defined as a natural tendency to create interpersonal conflict and disrupt social relations. This tendency is especially likely to erupt under pressure, and what is the biggest source of pressure and stress at work? Horrible bosses. So, you really need to have an enormous amount of self-control in order to hide your spontaneous feelings and true thoughts from your manager and suck up to him. As the French moralist Joseph Joubert noted, showing more love to people than they really deserve is kindness.

For some of us, it might not seem so hard to implement, but if you want to be truly successful in your career, then you need to work on being nice to people. Try to come across as considerate, warm, and caring, and *hide* your dark side tendencies from your colleagues and especially your boss. Arrogance never pays off, but kindness most certainly will, even though it often takes time—the top leadership scholars all agree on this, a rarity for academics. Jim Collins, author of *Good to Great*, pointed out in a seminal *Harvard Business Review* article that the best corporate leaders always combine intense professional dedication with extreme personal humility.[22] Collins's essay was deemed counterintuitive, but the only counterintuitive thing about it is that anyone could consider it counterintuitive. According to Collins, the key ingredients of top leadership are humility, will, and fairness (e.g., giving credit to others, assigning blame to oneself)—the exact opposite of arrogance.

Even more compellingly, Drs. Joyce Hogan and Robert Hogan have spent a combined fifty years studying the causes of successful and unsuccessful leadership, building a data archive of more than a million employees, most of them managers. Their results indicate unequivocally that the ability to get along with others is a deciding factor underlying promotion to managerial roles and, in particular, whether managers can genuinely lead an organization to success. People who are sensitive toward others get hired and promoted; people who are not get fired or destroy the organization.[23]

Finally, professor Timothy Judge, at the University of Notre Dame, analyzed leadership data from hundreds of independent research studies comprising thousands of managers; his results indicate that leaders tend to display more pro-social behaviors, such as being more agreeable and extroverted, and that those features are also more prominent in successful than unsuccessful leaders.[24, 25]

How to Boost Your Career Confidence (Even Though You Don't Have To)

In reality, wanting to boost your career confidence kind of misses the point. The most confident people I've known have been utterly unsuccessful in their careers, to the point of being virtually unemployable, despite being well educated and coming from rich families. Some were so confident that they felt entitled to some of the best jobs in the world (e.g., creative director of MTV, chief designer for Apple, and even lead singer of Coldplay), but they had neither the talent nor the work ethic to be worthy of such positions. Sadly for them, they kept their confidence intact and remained firm in their convictions that they should aspire to these top jobs, which stopped them from working on anything less ambitious and eventually made them completely unemployable, keeping them out of the job market for years. I suspect you also know people like this.

Our narcissistic society is full of people who have remarkably high career aspirations, combined with a rather low willingness to work or no natural talent to attain them. This combination results in people who are hard to manage—they become more and more arrogant, deluded, and bitter with the world. In his fascinating book, *The Blame Game*, business psychologist Ben Dattner points out that the members of Generation Y (people born in the eighties and nineties) are particularly prone to overrating their own career potential, which produces unmanageable expectations and an unrealistic sense of entitlement:

> Many of my baby boomer and Gen X clients have marveled to me that their younger employees seem to think that they deserve a gold star simply for showing up to work each day. My colleagues still recount the story of one new student, who asked during an orientation to the master's program, "What kind of job will I *receive* when I graduate?"[26]

Thus, too much career confidence is likely to hinder your career development, especially when your internal career confidence is high—in other words, when you believe your own hype. Indeed, your internal career confidence and your external career confidence each have different implications for your career success. As in other areas of competence, the only type of high confidence that is beneficial to your career is your external confidence, because it will increase the probability that you seem competent to others. On the other hand, your internal career confidence is actually more useful when it is low, manifested as the inner voice telling you that you should do better. Remember that you are the only person who hears and cares about that voice. Others are really not interested in your career confidence; all they want is to be able to assess whether you are competent or not, even if they often rely on your external confidence to do so, especially when they are not competent enough to distinguish between confidence and competence in others.

Demonstrating higher levels of competence to others will increase your career success, whereas demonstrating higher levels of competence to yourself will increase your career confidence. The former is a logical precondition for the latter. Genuine improvements in your career will usually translate into increases in your career confidence. Of course, your low career confidence may be unwarranted if you are too harsh on yourself or have a pessimistic bias. However, the way to deal with unrealistic low confidence (perfectionistic self-criticism) is no different from how you should deal with low realistic confidence, namely by boosting your competence. The only way to boost your career confidence without being delusional, then, is by actually being more successful. And to manage that, you need to boost your career competence—anything else will be pointless.

The bottom line is that you don't really have to boost your career confidence. In fact, lower confidence is advantageous for improving on the three key dimensions of employability: It prompts you to become more able (develop expertise), motivates you to work hard (to compensate for your perceived lack of competence), and minimizes the probability that you will act in a pompous and unlikable way.

Using It:

- Don't listen to the myths: Career success is not a function of self-belief, innate talent, or arrogance.

- Remember the most important attributes of successful corporate managers: trustworthiness, kindness, and empathy.

- Use colleagues past or present to help you get a sense of how you are perceived.

- Think of one of your favorite bosses or managers. How did she talk to you? How did she treat people, and are you able to emulate her behavior?

- Enhance your employability: Develop a strong résumé; ask others to proofread it and give their feedback. Practice interviews and giving presentations. Be proactive in becoming an expert!

- Develop a strong work ethic:
  —Preparation is key. The more you prepare, the less you underperform.
  —Think of ways to demonstrate your hunger to succeed and your get-up-and-go attitude to new colleagues or bosses. It might mean staying at work later than everyone else for the first few months, going the extra mile on an assignment, or even just little things like always being on time.

- Be likable:
  —Always be kind, even when this means showing someone a bit more compassion than he or she might deserve.
  —Be aware of your "dark side" tendencies and learn how to curtail them.
  —Give credit to those you work around and don't shy away from taking the blame sometimes.

- Embrace your internal low career confidence: Remember that this is what will drive you to always strive to be doing better.

5

Social Confidence and People Skills

> The ability to deal with people is as purchasable a
> commodity as sugar or coffee. And I will pay more for
> that ability than for any other under the sun.
>   —John D. Rockefeller (1839–1937)

How to Master Interpersonal Relations

Things haven't changed much since John D. Rockefeller's time:
Despite unprecedented technological advances, which have replaced a great deal of face-to-face interaction with digital communications, social skills are still the number one commodity on
our planet, not least because relationships, which depend entirely
on social skills, represent the foundation of any society.

This chapter will highlight the fact that, despite the importance
of social relations, most people are particularly bad at judging social
skills, both in themselves and in others. Contrary to what you may
believe, those who appear socially confident are often considered
cocky or arrogant and are more likely to fail in social situations. We'll
outline the benefits of low social confidence (namely, preventing embarrassment and humiliation, and motivating self-improvement), and
then we'll cover some simple guidelines for charming and influencing

others in social situations. As you've begun to see, focusing on others rather than yourself is a crucial pathway to success.

As with other domains of competence, people are especially delusional about their social skills when they feel very confident. A review of independent scientific studies reported an average correlation of .17 between people's self-perceived social skills—their confidence—and their actual social competence.[1] This suggests that people's insight into their own social skills is just marginally better than chance. In other words, a random score would be almost as indicative of our true social skills as our rational self-evaluation or self-knowledge is.

We are equally inept when it comes to judging others' social skills. For example, studies have shown that we are generally unable to tell whether others are lying, and the more confident we are in our ability to discriminate between truth and lies, the more likely we are to be wrong. In fact, the correlation between people's competence for detecting lies and their confidence in their ability to do so is virtually zero (.04, to be precise). It is therefore as reliable to base lie-detection judgments on chance as it is to trust your confidence. Alarmingly, this is true even for people who are in the business of spotting liars. For instance, law enforcement officers are as bad at identifying liars as laypeople are.[2]

Contrary to what you may think (and especially to what *they* tend to think), people with inflated social confidence do not perform better in social situations. There is no evidence for the beneficial effects of social confidence or the idea that feeling assertive in social situations will boost your performance or social competence.[3] In fact, the only measure by which socially confident people do better is their own assessment of their performance. I'm sure you know people who are very confident, secure, and dominant in social interactions. If you do, pay attention to how they evaluate their own performance (e.g., when they give a talk, go on a date, or pitch to a client). Ask them how they performed and they will tell you that they did exceptionally well, and, sadly, they really believe that's the case. Emphasis on "sadly" because it confers them no advantage, but quite a few disadvantages.

Psychologists Julia Bishop and Heidi Inderbitzen, from the University of Nebraska–Lincoln, asked five hundred ninth-grade pupils to nominate their most and least favorite classmates.[4] Each nominee was put into one of five categories, ranging from "popular" to "rejected." The researchers also obtained generic measures of confidence from all participants. Surprise, surprise (unless you've read the previous chapters), there was no correlation whatsoever between pupils' self-confidence ratings and their popularity as rated by their classmates. The only variable that differentiated people with lower and higher social confidence was whether pupils had a close friend in the class. Those who did rated themselves more favorably in popularity, which is understandable: They had at least one person who genuinely liked them in the class. But to assume that having a close friend is a sign of popularity is somewhat delusional, to say the least. In fact, if the rest of the world loved us as much as our closest friends do, we would experience far fewer insecurities and social anxieties than we do.[5]

Even from an early age, humans seem to misjudge their interpersonal skills. A group of psychologists asked teachers to assess the social skills, popularity, and classroom etiquette of their three hundred pupils, aged four to seven.[6] Teachers' ratings were totally unrelated to pupils' confidence ratings, which tended to be much higher. In another study, Dr. Duane Buhrmester and his team assessed the accuracy of students' self-rated competence vis-à-vis their roommates' ratings of them.[7] Again, there was no connection between how individuals viewed their own social skills and how they were viewed by their roommates. More confident students thought they were better in every domain of social competence:

> They claimed to be substantially better at initiating relationships, better at disclosing things about themselves, better at asserting themselves in connection with objectionable behaviors by others, better at providing emotional support to others, and significantly better even at managing interpersonal conflicts. The roommates' ratings told a very different story, however. For four of the five interpersonal skills, the correlation between self-rated self-esteem and roommate-rated skill fell short of significance, ranging from 0.01 for conflict management to 0.15 for assertion in the face of objectionable behaviors.[8]

The only domain in which confident students were actually rated more favorably was initiating new social contacts, but even then the correlation between confidence and competence was .38, suggesting only a small overlap between people's actual and self-perceived skills.

If anything, people who provide inflated self-ratings of social competence tend to be liked *less* by independent observers rather than more.[9] In short, there is *no* connection between social confidence and social competence, in particular for people who are confident about their own people skills. This begs the question of what role social confidence plays, especially if it is unlikely to have self-fulfilling effects by boosting one's social competence. The next section provides an answer to this question.

Social Confidence as Presentational Strategy

Given that we have little insight into our social competence, especially when we feel confident, psychologists have considered alternate interpretations of the role of confidence in relation to interpersonal skills. The overwhelming body of evidence suggests that rather than interpreting social confidence as insight into one's social competence, it seems more appropriate to interpret it as a preferred *self-presentational strategy*, or a put-on performance for our social encounters. Even when we think that our social confidence is an accurate representation of our ability to deal with others, notably strangers and new acquaintances, it is relevant only as a determinant of how other people see us. When our social confidence is high, we tend to persuade ourselves that others see us in a positive vein, which is not necessarily true. When our social confidence is low, we are usually realistic about the fact that others have an unfavorable impression of us. The main implication is that the relevant aspects of our social confidence are external; that is, our social confidence is first in the eye of the beholder, and then reflected into our own eyes—unless we are deluded.

There are two main types of presentational strategies we can use to impress and be liked or respected by others: high and low social confidence. If you are surprised about the idea that lower confidence can be successfully used to impress others, consider the following: The goal of low social confidence is not the pursuit of positive experiences, but the avoidance of negative ones, or what psychologists refer to as "avoidance goals," which actually encompass 50 percent of human goals.[10] It's an effective self-protective strategy against social embarrassment, rejection, humiliation, and failure.

Just as our confidence in any domain tends to fluctuate (at times, you feel more competent than at others), our social confidence is sometimes more focused on avoiding negative experiences than pursuing positive ones. As self-esteem expert Baumeister notes, sometimes we have to make a choice between a risk-averse strategy and a more risky approach that could pay off and improve our reputation. Baumeister gives the example of a public performance: We can choose to agree to the challenge (the riskier option, which may result in either losing face or gaining status) or to opt out and avoid potentially making a fool out of ourselves (the risk-averse strategy, which simultaneously eliminates the possibility of a beneficial outcome). Somebody using a high-confidence presentational strategy may be more likely to agree to the public performance, while an individual using a low-confidence presentational strategy may be more inclined to pass up the opportunity.[11]

The idea, then, is that high and low social confidence are indistinguishable in terms of their pursuit of desirable goals, except that low confidence leads to such pursuit via modest, low-key, and inhibited behaviors, whereas high confidence does so by unleashing a repertoire of dominant, assertive, and uninhibited behaviors. Interestingly, low social confidence is generally more effective than high social confidence, as people are better at avoiding embarrassment than gaining praise. In fact, there are three reasons why low social confidence should be preferred as a self-presentational strategy:

1. High social confidence raises others' expectations of our competence, whereas low social confidence lowers them. Indeed, low social confidence follows the "under-promise, over-deliver" principle, which is always preferable to "over-promise, under-deliver" (which emerges from high social confidence). Thus, low

social confidence puts less pressure on you and minimizes the probability that others will be disappointed.[12]

2. High social confidence increases the probability of making an erroneous (internal) prediction of our performance, which is both disconcerting and embarrassing. Failing to be as successful as we expected has two potential problematic consequences: making us realize that we were deluded about our competence, and producing a state of denial in which we don't accept that we were wrong. The former is a big blow to our confidence, but the latter poses a serious threat to our long-term social competence, particularly if we want to improve our social skills. The risk of finding ourselves in a situation in which we have to distort reality in order to avoid the unpleasant state of feeling more incompetent than we did can be minimized by simply presenting ourselves in a less confident manner. So, even if you are feeling confident, try to react to that confidence by adjusting your behavior in a way that makes you appear more modest and humble, and if you are not really feeling confident, don't force yourself to seem so. In general, it is better to be your own worst critic than to have others as critics while you think highly of yourself. Furthermore, even if you are acting a bit too modestly for your actual competence, others will probably let you know or treat you favorably—humility is much more valued than you think.

3. On the other hand, low social confidence presents a win-win situation. If it correctly predicts low social competence, we will at least feel competent about our forecast, which is a sign of social competence in itself. If, however, it turns out that we were overly pessimistic in our prediction, then we will be pleasantly surprised by the better-than-expected result, and feel

more competent than we did before. Thus, low social confidence helps us prepare for the worst while still allowing us to enjoy the benefits of success. As Dr. Baumeister and colleagues put it: "The humiliation of failure is intensified by prior boastful pronouncements, whereas it is diminished if one had predicted failure."[13]

In brief, although people with lower social confidence are as eager to please others as anyone else,[14] they tend to opt for risk-averse strategies in order to protect themselves from potential failures, while simultaneously increasing their chances of making a positive impact on others.

The Toxicity of High Social Confidence

Although few people realize it, there are big risks associated with high social confidence. As Baumeister and colleagues observe: "Describing oneself in glowing terms does not of course guarantee that others will end up regarding one favorably [because] there is the risk of appearing conceited and arrogant. Cultural norms prescribe against expressing highly favorable evaluations of oneself. Simply saying good things about oneself is associated with the risk of being viewed as a conceited braggart or in some similarly undesirable way."[15] The emphasis on cultural norms is important here because there is a great deal of cultural variability in the degree to which people accept displays of boasting.

As you can probably guess, Americans are more accepting of self-promotion than other nations, which is why you may find this section counterintuitive (and want to worry about your low social confidence). Narcissistic North American culture tolerates self-enhancement more than other societies do, hence the compelling nature of messages such as "just be yourself," "don't worry about what others think of you," etc. High self-confidence is a central value in the United States.[16] As we see, wherever we are, self-promotion is an ineffective strategy for getting others to like us or respect us. Most scientific studies in this area have been carried out with U.S. participants, and the evidence very clearly suggests that whatever confidence surplus people perceive (surpassing competence) is toxic. In other words, the minute people perceive that you have more confidence than competence, they like you less.

The simple facts are that self-promoters tend to be perceived as arrogant,[17] and people are much more likely to be admired, respected, and liked when they avoid self-claims of competence, in particular when others sing their praises. This is consistent with the common-sense idea that truly talented individuals can let their qualities speak for themselves.[18] Think about people who behave in a rude, socially inappropriate, aggressive, argumentative, uninhibited, or unempathetic manner, with no consideration for other people's feelings and no interest in pleasing others. Pick the first two examples that come to mind. Now think about whether they have low, average, or high confidence. . . . I bet you the royalties of this book that they are not in the low-confidence category. Clearly, then, higher confidence impairs social skills more than lower confidence does.

So we can see that while the popular view is that confidence is an important social booster that enhances our relationships with others, the reality could not be more different. Although confidence can be used to mask one's limitations and weaknesses, it is easier to do so by being modest and displaying low confidence. In fact, higher social confidence will be mistaken for competence only by those who are unable to judge competence, and even then it would be easier to get others to like you by avoiding blatant self-promotion and arrogance. The underlying logic to this argument is really quite basic: If you are competent, there's no need to enhance your talents with extra displays of assertiveness; if you are not, high confidence will only help you disguise it for a limited time with a limited number of people (who don't know any better anyway). Conversely, when competence is coupled with modesty and a splash of insecurity, you will be able to not just impress others but also gain their sympathy. The good news, if you have always felt somewhat unassertive and insecure in social situations, is that you will find it rather easy to avoid indulging in overt displays of confidence, so abstaining from toxic self-promotion will not be too difficult for you.

The Adaptive Side of Lower Social Confidence

William James argued that the most fundamental principle governing human behavior is our desire to be appreciated. This principle may be the single most insightful remark about social relations ever formulated. Anywhere in the world, our relationships are driven by a fundamental craving for acceptance and appreciation, and that will always be the case. At the same time, people differ in the degree to which they need acceptance from others, and the less confident you are in your ability to be accepted, the more effort you will make to achieve it. Or, if you prefer, you can reverse the roles. Think of *others* as the people who are trying to be accepted and liked by *you*. Now divide "others" into those with high and low confidence. . . . What do you get? Confident people who will work less hard to be accepted by you, and less confident people who are quite motivated to gain your acceptance. Thus William James's principle explains the inverse association between social confidence and social competence, as well as how lower social confidence can be a driver to produce higher social competence.

Who are the people who crave others' appreciation the most? The insecure. And what's the result of craving others' appreciation? Society. Indeed, any civilization is partly the product of our desire to please others, and it reinforces that desire with rules and norms. A simple quid pro quo or social exchange among its members: If you do something for others they will do something for you; if you are nice to others they will be nice to you. Ultimately, every manifestation of pro-social behavior is an attempt to improve how others see us and what others think of us. When we lack confidence, we feel that our chances of making a favorable impression on others are slim, which means that our social anxiety emerges from our perceived inability or incompetence to gain other people's affection, respect, and admiration.[19] Ultimately, low social confidence can always be interpreted as fear of being rejected or fear of relationship devaluation.

In line, there is a competitive element underlying low social confidence,[20] which is elicited in situations that lower people's confidence in their ability to attain the desired social status from others. Once again, it is easy to see the adaptive side of insecurity, this time in the form of low social confidence. Thus low social confidence is the result of either failing to fulfill your basic affiliation needs—the desire to connect or bond with others—or sensing that you won't be able to fulfill them. It is a signal that you are not as competent in social interactions as you would like to be, and that others fail to see in you the person you would like to be. Of course, it may be we are overly self-critical in our interpretations of how others see us, and that their views of us are not really that negative. However, it is better to err on the safe side and assume that we are not doing so well. As others are essential for the fulfillment of any goal, social confidence is a major aspect of confidence. Moreover, most low confidence in any domain is associated with the perception that we lack the power to alter other people's perceptions of us.

How to Use Your Low Social Confidence to Enhance Your Social Competence

There are three well-defined paths by which lower social confidence and even social anxiety (its extreme manifestation) can lead to increased social competence over time.

Path 1

PESSIMISTIC REALISM

We know that the reason for the near-zero correlation between social confidence and social competence is that confident people systematically overestimate how socially skilled they are. Conversely, people who are not assertive in social situations tend to be realistic about their skills deficit. Therefore, the first benefit conferred by lower social confidence is the ability to accurately assess your social competence. In other words, low social confidence is there to equip you with some *pessimistic realism*, or the ability to realize that you are not as strong interpersonally as you would like to be.

How do you realize this? By attending to negative feedback or disapproval signals from others, something confident people never do. Socially confident people tend to ignore any evidence suggesting that they may not be as popular as they hoped to be, to the point of distorting ambivalent evidence in order to reassure themselves that they are performing in a charming and desirable way in social situations. Less confident people are the exact opposite: They ignore evidence in support of their satisfactory performance to focus instead on the negatives. Sure, it can be quite painful to focus on the negative side of things—but that is also the only way you can deliberately improve on your performance and become more competent. Pay attention to your weaknesses, knowing it's OK to feel bad about them. If something is bothering you, then you should not pretend that you don't care, but rather do something about it.

Ironically, then, the pessimistic bias conferred by lower social confidence makes people more realistic, not least because the optimistic bias conferred by higher social confidence makes people delusional and much more unrealistic. As they say, "In the kingdom of the blind . . ."

Path 2

SELF-FOCUSED ATTENTION

Have you ever experienced the disinhibiting effects of alcohol? When we are mildly intoxicated (as opposed to very drunk) we experience the rather enjoyable and reassuring realization that although we may be embarrassing ourselves, we don't really care. In fact, alcohol consumption would probably drop substantially if it didn't produce the false sense of competence it does. It is useful to compare these effects to those of high social confidence: Drunkenness enables us to sing karaoke without inhibition at the office Christmas party or approach someone in a bar we would never approach when sober; likewise, high social confidence disinhibits us and unleashes our natural instincts. Great—or is it?

As anyone who has been forced to reexperience their own drunken antics while sober (perhaps via Facebook or YouTube) would realize, alcohol has no beneficial effects on social competence, other than the fact that others are often more forgiving and lenient with us when they realize that we are drunk. In addition, when we are drunk we are also less harsh on ourselves, but that isn't really an advantage. If boozing didn't reduce self-focused attention, people wouldn't do stupid things while drunk. That is the remarkable quality of sober-ness: It stops you from "being yourself" by imposing constant self-censorship on your behavior. You can think of low social confidence as a more extreme version of sobriety, and social anxiety as an even more extreme version of low social confidence. By the same token, alcohol tends to affect social competence by inflating our confidence to the point of embarrassment, even if we don't experience guilt and shame until we sober up. In short, lower confidence increases your preoccupation with what other people think of you, and that is a fundamental skill for functioning in society. Conversely, higher con-fidence inebriates you: You may feel more relaxed and loosen your inhibitions, but that's mostly to your own detriment. Be your own worst critic and you will avoid being criticized by others.

Path 3

MOTIVATION

Social anxiety (extreme low confidence) is not just a realistic signal that forces you to focus on your behavior to avoid making catastrophic impressions on others. It is also a driving force that motivates you to prepare, improve, and minimize embarrassment

ahead of daunting or challenging events. When you anticipate potential social failure (e.g., prior to a date, interview, exam, business
meeting, or presentation, all of which threaten your status with others), there is really only one coherent plan of action: prepare, prepare, and prepare.

Given that your low social confidence is likely to be an accurate
reflection of your low social competence—even when you are being
a bit harsh on yourself—it will drive social competence gains. Of
course, you could end up putting too much pressure on yourself, but
since when is that an impediment to getting better? When improvement goals are motivated by self-critical realism, people are much
better positioned to boost their competence than when they lack
self-criticism and are indifferent to failure. Although higher social
confidence may be beneficial during the performance stages, these
(slight) benefits are offset by the much more consequential lack of
preparation that precedes the performance of socially confident individuals. Conversely, the less confident you are, the more pessimistic your prediction of your performance will be, so it should trigger
even higher levels of preparation—and when you over-prepare, you
can even afford to underperform.

Think about the best students in school or college—they were
probably quite pessimistic in predicting how hard the exams would
be, and they probably worried a lot about failing. Because they worried so much, they were serious about studying. Or job applicants
preparing for an interview; or athletes going into an important competition; or artists preparing for an audition. In any domain of competence you can only turn your potential into high performance if
you are serious about your preparation, and your assessment of how
much you will need to prepare is inversely rather than positively
related to your confidence levels.

In the event that you want to ignore these paths to social competence or disregard the possibility that low social confidence confers an advantage in social relations, let me play devil's advocate for a moment: It is virtually impossible to deliberately boost your social confidence and switch from a pessimistic, damage-avoidance, and self-protective presentational style to an optimistic, reward-approach, self-enhancing presentational style. In plain English, this means that if you attempt to switch from low to high confidence in your approach to social relations, you will be quickly found out, and you will fail (even if you manage to fool others, you will most likely fail at persuading yourself). This is because your typical self-presentational style is the result of very early life experiences and even genetics.

Early Childhood Experiences Determine Your Social Confidence (and That's OK)

Sigmund Freud is credited with the idea that most of our adult behaviors are rooted in early childhood experiences. Most psychologists after Freud appeared to arrive at similar conclusions, even when they did not agree with the rest of his theories. This idea has clear implications for our understanding of social confidence: The tendency to be hyperalert to negative social outcomes, just like the opposite tendency to be fearless in social situations, develops at a very young age and cannot be easily changed after adolescence. It is one of the most compelling facts in psychology, and there's no reason to be dramatic about it. On the contrary, it is quite helpful to accept this. So, where does it all begin?

Before you are born, you inherit a predisposition to experience more positive or negative emotions. If you are generally socially anxious, it is because you are hypersensitive to threats and danger—this takes us back to the genetics of your brain. Although we cannot tell whether we've inherited more of our character from our mother or father, studies comparing genetically identical twins with fraternal twins (who share only 50 percent of their genes) show that genetic relatedness increases the probability of being similarly sensitive to threats and therefore similarly predisposed toward anxiety. In short, social confidence does have a genetic basis, even if that's just part of the story.

Soon after you are born, your inherited predisposition to interpret situations as more or less threatening influences your relationship with your caregiver (usually your mother). In turn, your caregiver tends to be more or less responsive to your emotional displays. The result is a typical pattern of the child-parent relationship, which consolidates within the first few years of life. As noted by Dr. Frances Vertue, author of a nifty theoretical essay on the subject, children develop steady beliefs and expectations about their parents and how other adults will treat them during their earliest interactions with their caregivers. These beliefs and expectations—often referred to as "working models"—tend to persist right through adulthood and influence how we interpret the world and our interactions with others (e.g., partners, friends, colleagues). Although our interpretations and "theories" may change, their core is still very much based on how we experienced our contact with our parents and other significant others as young children.[21]

As a result of the interaction between genetic factors and early childhood experiences, roughly 50 percent of people develop somewhat insecure internal models to interpret their social relations.[22] These models bias attention toward negative social signals and keep individuals alert to potential threats in order to help them avoid embarrassing situations and gain approval from others. There are three different ways of being cautious or pessimistic in your interpretation of social situations, all of which reduce your social confidence, though for the purpose of *boosting* your social competence! The first internal model, known as "fearful," is characterized by negative expectations about oneself and others. Fearful people are especially needy of others' reassurance, but they also find it hard to trust others. It is therefore no wonder that they approach social situations with low confidence. The second model, known as "preoccupied," characterizes people who question themselves but not others. Here, others' opinions are more effective at reducing one's self-doubts. The third model, "avoidant," is found in people who trust themselves but distrust others.[23] People with an avoidant internal model find it the hardest to bond with others because they are too independent and self-reliant for their own good.

It is important to note that the insecurities that may emerge from these three predispositions are often the cause of exceptional accomplishments. Indeed, in any domain of achievement you will find a large percentage of people who would not have achieved so much if they had been more secure or self-assured. And as we now know, success is often the only effective medication for your insecurities, in particular if they are accompanied by a genuine fear of failure. For example, one of the most successful entrepreneurs I ever met once confessed that failure is terrifying and brings about a feeling of embarrassment that is very difficult to handle. So to avoid this outcome, everything possible should be done to avoid the dreaded failure. Striving to be the best at everything is the safest way to ensure acceptance.

In short, given that your social anxiety emerges from fairly archaic and stable perceptions that you won't be able to make a desirable impression on others, and that those perceptions are usually right (minus, say, a 30 percent bias from your default internal model of interpretation), then all you have to do is work on improving your social skills and boosting your social competence. The next section explains how this can be done.

Turning Your Low Social Confidence into High Social Competence

We can all tell when someone is charming or annoying, but how do we know if someone is socially competent? By now, we know people are generally inept at assessing their own or others' social skills, so let's simplify it. There are only three fundamental elements of social competence; these are valid everywhere, at any point in time. First, social competence requires the ability to *read people*, exercising what some psychologists call "social knowledge." If you lack social knowledge, then you can't understand people—what they are doing, why they do what they do, what they mean when they say what they say, etc.—and you will struggle to function in any social situation. This is why we all feel handicapped when we arrive in a foreign country, especially when we don't speak the language or the culture is markedly different from ours. Second, and as already discussed, social competence involves successful self-presentation. More specifically, people with good social skills know how to *create a desired impression*, and they do it. Third and most important, social competence involves the ability to *influence others*—put simply, to get others to do what you want. This third element is hardly ever possible unless you conquer the first two.

In short: Social competence = reading others + presenting well + influencing others.

The trickier bit is putting this recipe into practice. If you manage two of the three elements in the formula you will be fairly successful in your relationships. If you manage all three then you will achieve exceptional success, and not just in social situations but also in your career. If you manage just one (or none) you will struggle in any domain of life. Let's dive into this in more detail, and consider the advantages and disadvantages of low social confidence for helping you strengthen your social competence in each of the three core domains of social skills.

Reading People Like a Book[24]

In simple terms, people who are better able to understand others are more socially astute and should therefore have an advantage when it comes to dealing with others. In fact, knowing others is not just more important than knowing yourself; it is also the only way you can know yourself in the first place—because others are better able to judge you and assess your competence than you are yourself; that is, your reputation is in the eyes of others. So, how can you improve your understanding of other people and use it to your own advantage? Simple. By knowing what others want. So, what do people want? Why, the same three things as you:

> Love (being appreciated and valued by others)
> Success (status or the achievement of one's goals, as well
>   as competence gains that are recognized by others)
> Knowledge (understanding the world and feeling in con-
>   trol of it)

These three *master motives* apply to people in any society any-where, and they are the most fundamental building blocks for any interaction with others.[25] The bottom line is that people want exactly the same things you want. Would you be reading this book if you didn't want to improve your understanding of confidence (knowledge), and use that to improve your relationship with others (love) and boost your achievements (success)? I hope not.

Astute Self-Presentation

Anybody is capable of displaying social competence—think about how you behave when you are with close friends, or family members you don't dislike: That's you at your *smartest* from a social point of view. Why? Because you successfully communicate your inner self or identity to others. In other words, you manage to get others to see the person you would like them to see in you, which is the same person you see when you are satisfied about yourself. Astute self-presentation is the "processes by which people negotiate identities for themselves in their social worlds. In the privacy of one's own mind, perhaps, one may be relatively free to imagine one-self having any sort of identity, but serious identity claims generally require social validation by other people, and so the construction of identity requires persuading others to see one as having desired traits and qualities."[26]

Luckily, the vast majority of our social interactions occur with people who are close to us, such that we spend around 80 percent of the time relating to 20 percent of the people we know and 20 percent of the time relating to the remaining 80 percent (which includes strangers and one-time acquaintances). For instance, even though people have hundreds of "friends" on Facebook, most of their interactions are with just five or six people, which is roughly the number of intimate friends anyone has at any point in their lives.[27] Predictably, intimacy depends on how frequently we interact with people—we only truly bond with people if we see them often, even if it's just on Facebook.[28]

We all have people who like us and who make us feel comfortable. The key challenge is to generate the same effect with strangers, to feel as relaxed with and valued by people who are not as close to us, not least because it will provide an opportunity to get close to them. What is upsetting, then, is *not* being able to present ourselves to new acquaintances as we do to those who know us and like us.

We all hope to create a public persona that supports our preferred beliefs about ourselves, because a successful reputation is the ultimate antidote to self-deception: "It is hard to believe oneself to be brilliant, glamorous, and attractive if everyone else regards one as mediocre on all."[29] The most likely function of low social confidence is to encourage you to engage in what psychologists refer to as "controlled" self-presentation. This means that lower confidence increases your willingness to manipulate your presentational style in order to enhance your reputation—precisely to compensate for your perceived low social competence. By the same token, people who feel very confident don't pay much attention to this and act just like they naturally feel, which means disregarding others' impressions. Think about a situation in which you were trying to make a favorable impression on someone (e.g., a date or making a new acquaintance). Chances are that if you were focusing on coming across in a positive way, you were not really that confident about achieving this; therefore, you sought out instant feedback cues in order to adjust your behavior—for example, by making sure you didn't say anything the other person would dislike.

In line, leading scholars in social competence research have recently proposed that the essence of self-presentation is a form of *interpersonal self-control*, or the capacity to demonstrate high levels of self-control in public social contexts.[30] Those better able to control themselves will make a better impression on others and in turn be better able to manage others. Furthermore, those with low social confidence appear to be more modest, which is appealing to others, as we've learned.[31] This "willingness" is actually the default presentational strategy of unassertive people, and contrary to the cliché idea that an unassertive image is a tragic one to convey (the dominant view of any narcissistic society), modest people are actually liked more than dominant or extremely confident people are (even in America). Quite right, then, that lower social confidence censors the more confident and unrepressed presentational style we adopt when we are with close friends and family, the only people who are happy to put up with our "genuine" selves.

Be strategic about the information you choose to convey to others. People want to see the best possible version of you and, ideally, someone they can predict consistently; it adds to their sense of control and enables them to fulfill their own knowledge motive. Thus, astute self-presentation involves being predictable—consistent—to others; if you are unpredictable, people freak out.

All this being said, try not to focus too much on how best to present yourself to others. Indeed, a moderate degree of social anxiety is no doubt conducive to higher social competence, but too much of it can impair your performance by overloading your mind and riddling you with hesitations. Whether you are speaking in public, performing in front of others, or meeting new people, what you want to achieve is a healthy balance between displaying the set of behaviors or communicating the ideas you had in mind (as originally planned) and responding to people's feedback as you see fit. For example, whenever I'm giving a talk to a big audience, I make sure that I have a small list of two or three messages I should definitely convey, and my attention is split between executing that task and monitoring people's reactions to what I say. However, if I spent too much time focusing on what other people were doing, I would forget to convey the messages, which would harm my presentation. As noted by University of Florida psychologists Beth Pontari and Barry Shlenker,[32] who studied the effects of mental effort on self-presentation, if you're socially anxious, you may be constantly preoccupied by thoughts of how others are seeing you. The high level of self-awareness that accompanies social anxiety will tend to bring about a negative self-view, whereby you focus mostly on your negative qualities and limitations. Getting too caught up in these concerns can distract you from the situation you're in and the task at hand, which includes making a good impression on those you're with.

Studies have shown that less confident individuals display greater social skills when they are given a distracting task, which stops them from focusing too much on making a good impression. It's a bit like counting sheep when you are trying to fall asleep—occupying your mind with a trivial task helps you switch off from more persistent and obsessive thoughts. When you are extremely motivated to achieve something, your mind can go into overdrive, which, ironically, is counterproductive, as these negative evaluative concerns may have the net result of facilitating a challenging self-presentation. The obsessive negative thoughts that accompany social anxiety may be replaced by those of the distracting task.[33] So, make a list of potential distractions (ideally, goals you want to accomplish) and keep your mind on that list, albeit making sporadic "checks" on what other people may be thinking.

Influencing Others

Assuming you are able to present yourself in a positive vein *and* read other people, you will be able to execute the final and most crucial step needed to display high social competence—namely, influencing other people. In order to understand how best to influence others, it is not necessary to inspect any groundbreaking research findings or social media trends. People have barely changed in the past hundred years—they remain interested in love, knowledge, and status. These goals are universal and so are the principles of human influence. Let's recall the words of the wisest of social influence experts, Dale Carnegie. In his book *How to Win Friends and Influence People*,[34] Carnegie outlines a list of practical suggestions to enhance our ability to influence people; here are some of my favorite ones:

1. *Only fools criticize.* Although it may be tempting to criticize others, that is only the "half-smart" option. Indeed, we tend to criticize others because we think that they are wrong and we are right. However, it is a lot more important to understand why others think what they think; once we manage to do so, we will give up on the idea of criticizing them. Moreover, 99 percent of the time there is no clear right or wrong, but multiple possibilities. It follows that in the vast majority of cases, no matter how strongly you feel that you are right, you may actually not be more right than other people who have seemingly opposed points of view.

2. *Avoid complaining.* Just as it is easy to criticize, it is easy to complain. But there are two big problems with this: First, you will irritate others; second, you will also irritate yourself. Learn to accept the fact that things aren't perfect and you will come to terms with everyday problems. Not everything can be as you want it to be, and you cannot control certain things. However, one thing you *can* control is your tendency to complain—and if you do so you will feel less irritated and be more popular with others (whether they are friends, work colleagues, or family).

3. *Give honest compliments to people.* It is the only thing others want to hear. Most people cannot deal with criticism. Every person craves appreciation and positive feedback. Find a way to compliment others sincerely and they will enjoy your company and like you. Do not make stuff up, though. Praising others will only work if they believe that you believe in them—so make sure that you spend sufficient time identifying others' strengths, and be sure to make them the focus of the conversation.

4. *Get others to want what you want.* The only way to get someone to do something is to get that person to *want* to do something. This is the cornerstone of motivation: The only motivation that counts is self-motivation, so all we can do to influence others' behavior is motivate *them* to do something. Most people fail at this because they simply cannot see the other person's point of view. Try to see the world from other people's point of view and you will understand what makes them tick and how you can make them tick.

5. *Be interested in others.* That's what they hope for. As most people are self-centered, it is rare to find people who pay attention to others. This leaves most of us craving others' attention. If

you show an interest in others (e.g., asking them questions, making them the center of the conversation, and most important, paying attention to what they say and do), you will charm them.

6. *Smile.* It never fails, and it is so easy to implement. There is no easier, quicker, more effective way to make others like you than to smile. People who smile more frequently are seen as more trustworthy, warmer, more socially skilled, and even more attractive. And you have total control over this: Smiling is a deliberate behavior and if you are struggling to find a way of doing it naturally, then just think of something fun.

7. *Remember people's names.* A person's name is the most treasured word he or she has. Knowing it is an easy and quick way to demonstrate you care about someone (most people forget others' names but everybody wants others to remember theirs).

8. *Listen.* Everyone can talk, but few people listen. If you think about it, it should be a lot easier to listen than to talk, yet people's propensity to do more talking than listening suggests otherwise. Unsurprisingly, good listeners are in high demand, but there is a surplus of people who talk.

9. *Get others to talk (while you listen).* It will make you more likable because you will make others the center of attention (instead of competing with them). In addition, getting others to talk about themselves is a good way of showing interest in them—something most people don't do.

10. *Talk about what other people like.* See the world as they see it (or at least try). If you only see the world from your point of view, you will never be able to understand other people, or even yourself. Start seeing things from other people's viewpoint

and you will get a four-dimensional view of the world, including yourself!

11. *Show that you value and even admire others.* No matter who they are or how important they are, they will never refuse the chance to be recognized. Indeed, important people will feel offended if you don't make them feel important, and relatively unimportant people will feel flattered (and be pleasantly surprised) when you make them feel important. Either way, then, it's a win-win situation.

12. *Don't argue.* The only way to win an argument is to avoid it. Most of us are quick to jump into disputes, especially when we feel that we are right. However, nobody likes to be proven wrong. Therefore, your ability to avoid arguments will not just save you energy; it will save you from confrontation, which will make you more popular and free up time and resources for more important activities. Avoiding confrontation also allows the other person to save face—in an argument, you will either lose or you will defeat him and cause him embarrassment. By avoiding arguments, you can avoid both of these outcomes.

13. *Respect people's opinions.* Don't tell people that they are wrong, especially when they are. William James once noted that truth is just something that happens to an idea. In other words, ideas are just ideas but sometimes they are also defined as being "true." This definition, however, depends on people's points of view, and the proof of this is that the same idea can be true at some point and false at another.

14. *When you are wrong, admit it.* It will make up for any mistake. People will forgive most things if you accept responsibility

and blame yourself seriously enough. So, even if you are not completely convinced that you may be wrong, it is better to admit it than deny it.

15. *Always start by giving positive feedback.* Praise is like the anesthetic used by dentists before they start drilling into your teeth. Always emphasize the positives first, and then slowly move to the negatives, but finish up on a high note.

16. *Make others say yes.* They will persuade themselves that you think like they do (which would imply that you are great!). This technique has proven quite effective in sales and is commonly known as the "foot-in-the-door" method; the salesperson starts by making small requests to which the customer can easily agree.

17. *Let others take credit for your ideas.* This will make people feel special, and few things are more counterproductive than denying someone a little boost to her self-esteem when she seems to crave it. Furthermore, few people are genuine creators of ideas—mostly, we all seem to forget where our ideas come from. As the great Albert Einstein once noted, creativity consists primarily of the ability to hide our sources (not just from others but also from ourselves).

18. *Praise from the bottom of your heart.* Try to always find a reason for complimenting others. To emphatically compliment people is to make them feel good—and when you make others feel good you will almost certainly make them like you. Although some people may seem unworthy of your compliments (think, for instance, of people you really dislike), with a bit of imagination and a good incentive it is easy to find one or two virtues to

highlight in others. And if you do this you will not just make others like you but also entice them to behave in the most positive of ways, which will make *them* more likable, too. Thus compliments are like self-fulfilling prophecies: Even if they are not 100 percent true when stated, if you state them sincerely and persuasively they will become true!

19. *Give people a good reputation to live up to.* This is probably the best single piece of advice regarding social skills ever given (and a summary of several key points in this book). Since our reputations depend on others—i.e., your reputation is whatever people think of you—we can influence people's identity (how they view themselves) by shaping their reputations. Tell a child that he is a nice boy and he will act accordingly; tell him he is a bad boy and he will misbehave. And the same occurs with adults. We all have strengths and weaknesses, but when we hang out with people who highlight our weaknesses they bring us down; in contrast, spending time with people who are focused on our strengths makes us feel stronger and better.

Almost a century after the formulation of Carnegie's social competence rules, psychologists are still in agreement with him. Indeed, recent studies show that social competence is best understood as a combination of social responsiveness, social maturity, and social control.[35] Social responsiveness is about expressing warmth and interest in others—clearly, cocky people are less likely to do this than humble, modest, and even underconfident people. Social maturity involves controlling negative emotions and appreciating others, as well as tolerating people who are different from us. Finally, social control refers to the motivation to improve one's social skills to influence others—again, your motivation will be higher if you perceive that you lack social competence.

More important, each of Carnegie's principles will be easier to implement for people with *lower* rather than higher social confidence. People who see themselves as more desirable and attractive may be more likely to strike up conversations with strangers, but that's where their advantage ends. In fact, after that, higher confidence increases the likelihood of behaving in a socially undesirable manner, as it is much more likely to result in arguments, self-centeredness, and arrogant behavior.

Using It:

- Relationships form the foundation of our society, but most people are inept at judging social skills (both their own and others').

- Having more social confidence does not equate with being more socially competent. There is no correlation between social confidence and actual social competence as rated by others. If anything, being overconfident in your social skills tends to mean others will like you *less*.

- Social confidence can be used as a presentational strategy, in the forms of both high and low confidence. The strategy of low confidence often leads to better outcomes, as it lowers others' expectations of us, and it enables us to make more realistic predictions of our performance and to be pleased when we are then able to fulfill these predictions. It also prevents us from coming across as arrogant or conceited, which is socially undesirable.

- Our relationships and interactions are driven by the intense need to be appreciated, particularly if we are unconfident and fear rejection from others. But if we let our low social confidence alert us to the fact that we are not as socially competent as we would like to be, it can be a driving force behind our working to improve.

- Low social confidence, and even social anxiety, can lead to increased social competence, through:
  —Pessimistic realism: the ability to accurately assess your social skills by paying attention to feedback in order to identify and work on your weaknesses.
  —Self-focused attention: When you have low social confidence, you pay a lot of attention to yourself and how you're doing. If you're preoccupied with what others think of you, you can identify and overcome the weaknesses for which they may criticize you.
  —Motivation: Social anxiety drives you to improve in order to avoid an undesirable outcome. If you are more afraid of failing, you will be more likely to prepare and do better.

- Low social confidence develops early in life, as a result of both genetics and early childhood experiences. But any fear you feel should not be seen as a bad thing—let it motivate you to work as hard as you can to achieve your goals.

To improve your social competence, you need to learn how to *read people* (know that they want love, success, and knowledge), *create a desired impression* (get people to see you in the way you want to be seen, but without getting too caught up in focusing on your limitations), and *influence others* (make a concerted effort to appreciate, show an interest in, and get along with other people).

6

A Loving Relationship

The greatest happiness of life is the conviction that we are loved—loved for ourselves, or rather, loved in spite of ourselves.   —Victor Hugo (1802–1885)

How to Boost Your Dating Confidence

L et us now look at the issue of dating confidence. If you are reading this, you are more likely to have low dating confidence (whatever your relationship status may be). If that is the case, you probably envy people who come across as confident when flirting with others or interacting with their romantic partners. It may not surprise you by now to know that boosting your confidence will do very little to improve your relationship success. In fact, the real issue is not how to become more confident—many people in the world feel as eligible as Angelina Jolie and Brad Pitt and yet they spend their lives being single or in unrewarding relationships—but how to become more competent at dating and romantic relationships. This chapter makes three main points:

1. There is a big difference between dating confidence and dating competence, which most people ignore.

2. Your low dating confidence can help you increase your dating competence (don't worry, I will tell you how).

3. There is a time to fake dating confidence, because it will enhance your dating competence.

I am confident that this chapter will equip you with the necessary know-how to attain the romantic success you desire. All your dating insecurities represent the very raw ingredients you will need to become a more attractive, eligible, and competent dater. The more convinced you are that you are not a good catch, the more this chapter will help you. In other words, the lower your dating confidence, the more you will improve your dating competence, and the more confident you will feel in turn about your dating competence. Ready?

Dating Confidence Is Not Dating Competence

Have you ever wondered why some people are more eligible (deemed more attractive dating partners) than others? I have been studying this issue for more than a decade now, and I still feel like I can't give you a short answer, but I'm going to try anyway: Because they have more desirable features. Too abstract? OK, let me break down the "desirable features" into physical and psychological. Most of the physical features are rather obvious and can be summed up in one word: *looks*. Some people like to think that beauty is in the eye of the beholder, but that is not true. Sure, there are subtle variations in taste, but within specific cultures most people agree on who is more and who is less attractive. People often discuss and even rate other people's attractiveness. For those cases we do not discuss, 90 percent of our attractiveness ratings would fall in the same "zone,"[1] showing that beauty is not really in the eye of the beholder.

Next comes the tricky bit—the *psychological* features of attractiveness. Why is this one harder to judge? Because compared to looks, the psychological determinants of eligibility are much more subjective. Most people find others more attractive when they seem smart, but having a smart partner is more important to women than to men, even in egalitarian societies. Women are also more attracted to men of higher social status (i.e., money, class, and power), but the rest is pretty arbitrary. Extroverts are sometimes rated more attractive than introverts, and friendly women tend to be perceived as better potential partners than aggressive ones. When it comes to values (beliefs, attitudes, and preferences), criteria are rather variable, though the short story is the rather predictable finding that couples who share values tend to be happier and have longer relationships.

Both women and men value looks more than any psychological trait, which is why we tend not to be interested in finding out about the personality of online daters unless they also include pictures of themselves in their profiles. Once we find someone attractive enough, we start paying attention to what they are like: Are they nice, smart, fun, and, finally, "compatible" with us? As for confidence, women tend to prefer men who seem more confident, but only when they interpret that confidence as a sign of actual competence. Men, on the other hand, appear not to care about a woman's confidence. While some may be put off by a woman who comes across as insecure and needy, if she is thought to be sufficiently eligible (especially in terms of her attractiveness), most men will happily ignore this lack of confidence.

Scientific studies also expose a clear gap between people's

self-rated eligibility and how eligible they actually are (what others think of them). For example, most people believe their relationships are happier than average, which is logically impossible. Likewise, most people assume that their partners are more eligible than they actually are, which is an indirect way of overrating their own dating competence.

Marsha Gabriel and her colleagues at the University of Texas[2] tested the relationship between self-rated and actual attractiveness in a sample of 150 college students. As expected, self-ratings of attractiveness were totally unrelated to participants' actual attractiveness. In fact, adjusting for chance (simply guessing one's attractiveness score) fewer than two in ten participants were able to accurately estimate their attractiveness level as reliably assessed by independent raters.[3] In most cases, people's inability to know how attractive they were resulted from their optimistic delusion that they were more attractive than others. This was especially true for males. In fact, the only women who overrated their attractiveness were narcissistic, whereas all men (not just narcissists) tended to overestimate theirs. Despite this sex difference, narcissism levels were the most important determinants of delusional self-ratings of attractiveness for the whole sample, which implies that the more dissatisfied you are with yourself, the more realistic you are about your own attractiveness level. Thus low dating confidence is a realistic symptom of low dating competence, but high dating confidence is almost certainly indicative of a self-deceptive bias. This is in line with Dr. Baumeister's seminal review of the self-esteem literature, in which he states that in contrast to any kind of objective measures, individuals with high self-esteem tend to make delusional claims about their high likability, attractiveness, and even strength of their relationships.[4]

This inability of people to obtain accurate ideas about their own attractiveness is a real shame, since it implies that the majority are unaware of how potential partners really see them. Furthermore, given that attractiveness plays a crucial role in determining anyone's eligibility, a discrepancy between one's self-rated and actual attractiveness will cause a big gap between how eligible one thinks one is and how eligible one *really* is. Consider the implications of living in a world where the vast majority of people think they are better looking than they actually are. Thinking that you are a better catch than you are does not make things easier; it makes them harder.

A few years ago, I got my first job as a professional matchmaker, when the UK-based TV series *Dating in the Dark*[5] hired me to interview, test, and match contestants. If you haven't seen the show, all you need to know is that three men and three women are sent to a big house where they are allowed to interact with the opposite sex in only one of the rooms, which is pitch-black. For the rest of the time, the women live in one part of the house, the men in another. Whenever they want to meet, they have a blind date, literally—they can talk, play, eat, drink, touch, and kiss, but the lights remain switched off, so they experience each other without seeing each other. After a few days each contestant is allowed to choose *one* date to see face-to-face, and decide whether they would continue dating that person once the show is over. In the real world, looks are the first thing we are exposed to, and we only get to find out what other people are like after deciding whether we find them physically attractive or not. Consequently, looks influence our judgment of people's character. In *Dating in the Dark*, however, people are first exposed to others' psychological traits, so they judge their personality, values, and attitude "purely"—that is, without being influenced by looks. This makes the show a genuine psychological experiment.

Given that the contestants report whether they are interested in others before *and* after they see what they look like, the show is a great vehicle for testing the relative importance of psychological factors (personality) vis-à-vis physical factors (looks). In fact, *Dating in the Dark* provides an excellent opportunity to test people's awareness of their eligibility. Some may be confident about their appearance but find their personality a bit more problematic; others may feel they are a good emotional or intellectual match for others but feel less confident about their appearance, etc. At the same time, ratings of competence—how eligible *others* find you—can be obtained before and after looks are revealed, enabling us to measure psychological and physical attractiveness separately. In other words, the format of the show made it possible to test the relationship between confidence and competence for both physical and psychological determinants of dating eligibility.

Unsurprisingly, and in line with the findings of Dr. Gabriel's study, most daters were completely unaware of their eligibility, both in terms of their looks and personality. Daters who rated themselves high on attractiveness were generally deemed unattractive by their potential dates. The vast majority of daters who thought they had a great sense of humor were not considered funny. And almost all contestants—male and female—who described their conversation as "interesting" were considered boring or obnoxious by their potential dates. Moreover, the more delusional people were about their looks and charms, the less likely they were to leave the show with a date. Indeed, the relationship between contestants' confidence in their ability to be perceived as a desirable dating candidate by other contestants was *inversely* related to their actual success rate.

Although *Dating in the Dark* included contestants from all ages

and backgrounds—rich, poor, white, black, young, old, you name it—
there was one aspect on which they were not representative of the
wider population; namely the fact that they were so desperately looking for a romantic partner. These daters were therefore already less
competent than the average dater from the general population, which
includes people who have found a partner, as well as those who are in
fulfilling relationships, etc. Yet in looking at how confident contestants were, you would have never guessed they were unsuccessful.

In my career I have spoken to many people with relationship
issues, and the single most common cause of their problems is lack
of self-awareness. That is, these people are either unaware of how
their behavior affects others—for example, their partners—or unaware of how desirable or undesirable they may be to others. Indeed, even when people have a track record of relationship failures,
their experiences appear to have very little or no effect on their self-
perceived dating competence. When you compare the average confidence levels of people who are in successful relationships with
those who are not, there is little difference between them, and the
main reason is that the latter think they are more eligible than they
actually are. It should come as no surprise that people's propensity
to overrate their dating competence is inversely related to their ability to succeed at finding someone.

Sometimes, then, confidence is not just different from competence but also its opposite. This applies to people who overrate their
dating potential, as well as those who deem themselves less eligible
than they actually are. The good news is that low dating confidence
is a lot easier to fix than high confidence. In fact, feeling insecure
about your eligibility will help you become more eligible. The next
section explains just how.

Four Ways to Succeed in Romantic Relationships

If you want to be more successful in your romantic relationships, you don't need to worry about boosting your confidence—that will come as a natural result of improving your love life. You might say that you could be grateful to your low confidence for driving you in the direction of positive change. Often, the most serious relationship problem people have is the unwillingness or inability to recognize the issue at hand. In contrast, when you are unhappy about your dating situation, you have already solved 50 percent of your problem. There are four main reasons for failing to find or maintain a happy relationship.

1. Aiming too high (unrealistic expectations)
2. Aiming too low (being satisfied with anything and anyone)
3. Being overly logical or mathematical in your assessment of what you need
4. Thinking that finding the right partner guarantees a perfect relationship

Confidence is related to all of the above. Overconfident people aim higher than they should, which keeps them single. Underconfident people aim lower than they should, which keeps them in unrewarding relationships. Being too mathematical in your assessment of what you need can result from either under- or overconfidence: not having sufficient confidence in your spontaneous emotions and impulses, or having too much confidence in your ability to rationally calculate what you need. Finally, the illusion that there is a Mr. or Ms. Right waiting for you somewhere, and that finding him or her will guarantee you effortless relationship happiness, is the consequence of having more confidence in that imaginary person than in yourself (or anyone else you may be dating). Avoiding these four relationship pitfalls will help you improve your love life. Now let's look at the four ways of boosting your relationship success:

1.   Don't aim too high → Aim lower
2.   Don't aim too low → Aim higher
3.   Don't be too rational → It is OK to go with the flow
4.   Don't hope for perfection → Work on improving what you have

Let's look at these recommendations in more detail.

Don't Aim Too High → Aim Lower

Aiming lower is easy, but *wanting* to aim lower can often be difficult, especially if you don't understand why. The easiest way to aim lower is to give people you may not instantly like a chance. It is also important that you don't spend too much time without dating anyone—opportunities don't just arrive; you have to create them. So, don't be too strict, and loosen your criteria. Even if you have five key boxes your ideal romantic partner should tick, go for people who may only tick two or three of those boxes, and see how it goes. It often takes some time until the best qualities in people are revealed, and this is especially true for people who may not seem as eligible as they actually are.

It is often the case that no matter how eligible you are, if you are single despite wanting to be in a relationship, you may well have been aiming too high. Although a somewhat unflattering comparison, think about someone who has been trying to sell a car or a house for years—even when the market is down, anything can be sold for the right price. The same applies to relationships and dating—if you keep waiting for someone better, you could end up waiting forever. Although this could perpetuate a vicious circle, the problem *should* end up fixing itself, by forcing you to adjust your expectations. Indeed, while overconfidence increases your chances of remaining single, the longer you are single the *less* confident you should become, and your ratings of eligibility will be more realistic. Unfortunately, it often takes too long to reach this stage. The unconscious desire to maintain high dating confidence often causes people to be delusional and to not accept the truth. These people are unable to adjust their self-ratings of eligibility in accordance with reality, due to their overconfidence. It is *lower* confidence that helps to build realistic ratings of eligibility and consequently increase dating success.

It is not uncommon for people with high standards to overcompensate for their lower (inner) confidence by pretending that nobody is good enough for them. In doing so, they attempt to project confidence to others, conveying the message that they are too eligible for most people. In reality, this attitude simply reflects the insecurities of not being confident enough to settle with a potential partner who may be criticized by others.

Contrary to popular belief, research indicates that there is no association between choosiness and eligibility. In fact, the effects of higher choosiness on dating success are often negative, because dating success ends up depending on seducing fewer, more sought-after candidates, who, in contrast, have many interesting choices available. For example, one of my clients spent ages being single despite being highly eligible. She was attractive, charming, and socially competent, and she had a glamorous job. Yet after breaking up with her childhood sweetheart at the age of twenty, she remained single until she was thirty-five, becoming increasingly picky and hard to please. Whenever she met someone who appeared good enough for her—which didn't happen very often—he turned out to be just not that interested in her, not least because he had many other options, whereas my client kept reducing her range of choices by becoming ever more choosy instead of "lowering the asking price." In a recent study, Mitja Back, from the Johannes Gutenberg University Mainz, studied the behavior, beliefs, and preferences of 382 single people who attended a speed-dating event (where they can spend up to three minutes with each candidate before moving on to the next).[6] Unlike in real world dating, speed dating allows everyone to date everyone, enabling researchers to take a rigorous look at the determinants of choice and success in dating. Accordingly, Dr. Back's team gathered data on participants' choices, and assessed their confidence in being chosen by more as well as less eligible partners, which they interpreted as an indicator of self-perceived eligibility.

The study found, unsurprisingly, different results for men and women. Eligible men tended to be pickier, because they could choose from a wider range of women. However, there was no relationship between eligibility and choosiness among women, such that ineligible women tended to be as choosy as their eligible counterparts. Putting these findings together, it is easy to understand why being choosy is problematic for women: Not only does it constrain their options (to fewer men); the men they are likely to choose may easily find someone who is both more eligible and less choosy, as well as many other women who are as eligible and less choosy. A woman who aims too high, then, is driving into a dating cul-de-sac. Dr. Back and colleagues also found that the probability of being chosen by the person daters chose was only marginally better than chance, or being chosen by anyone else in the group. This led the authors to conclude that "people expect their mate choices to be reciprocal but generally, they are not."[7]

Don't Aim Too Low → Aim Higher

This advice is not so much for people who find themselves usually single, but for those who drift from one relationship to the other. My client Silvia (not her real name) has spent the past twenty years going from one relationship to the next, with no more than a couple of weeks of being single in between. Confidence plays an important role here: Being obsessed with avoiding singlehood is indicative of a lack of confidence in being alone, as if your self-worth depended on being in a relationship. Big mistake. This approach hardly ever pays off, since you end up "selling yourself too cheaply" and jumping into new relationships without really being emotionally or mentally ready. So, if you are a systematic dater and have spent more time with someone than alone, you should follow the advice in this section.

It may be that being single makes you feel unhappy about yourself, but it will also enable you to invest in the right relationship when a suitable candidate arrives. If you are worried about what others think of you, then you should know that they will be more likely to criticize you for being with someone unworthy of you than for being alone (besides, if they are your true friends then they will just care about your being happy).

When you go to a restaurant, you don't randomly order something from the menu. When you go to the movies, you don't arbitrarily pick any film. Choosing somebody to spend the rest of your life (or a considerable amount of it) with should require some thinking. Moreover, if your need to constantly be with someone results merely from your desire to feel good about yourself—because your self-worth depends on having a partner—you will need to find someone who can actually make you feel accomplished, which is not going to be easy if you are punching below your weight.

Regardless of how attractive, funny, wealthy, or sexy you are, some people will be inadequate matches for you, so why not avoid them? Dating is neither a lottery nor a charity. If you are with someone who is as eligible as you, the relationship will be more likely to work, and you will feel better about it. If you are with someone who is less eligible than you, you will sooner or later come to the conclusion that you could have done better. Aiming higher does not necessarily mean being with someone as attractive, funny, wealthy, or sexy as you, but he or she should at least be a good match overall.

So, how do you work out how eligible you are? The best and quickest way is to ask people who will give you honest feedback—for example, close friends, relatives, or previous partners (if you're still on speaking terms!). If you want a simple scientific formula, your overall eligibility is a combination of four factors:

1. Looks: what evolutionary psychologists call "fitness"
2. Brains: how smart and resourceful you are
3. Partner potential: whether you will be loyal, loving, caring, and good company
4. Parenting potential: whether you will be a good mother or father

Although your partner's eligibility depends on exactly the same criteria, women tend to value brains and partner potential more than men do, and men tend to value looks and parenting potential more than women do. If it has always been easy to find a partner, you are probably underestimating your eligibility compared with your partner's, or you just haven't been patient enough to wait for someone who is your match. Either way, the underlying issue is that you are not feeling confident enough in your ability to find a better partner, which means that it is time to improve your dating confidence. How? Start aiming higher—you will probably succeed.

Don't Be Too Rational → It Is OK to Go with the Flow

Few people have spent more time coming up with matchmaking formulas than I have, and 99.9 percent of the people in the world are more skeptical about the degree to which such formulas work than I am. The disappointing truth, however, is that the "science" of love is still very much a work in progress. Let me give you an example. If we could test two people for an entire week, forcing them to complete hours of psychological tests, interviewing them about their values, preferences, and hobbies to find out precisely what it is that they are looking for, and even obtaining readings of their DNA, our scientific evaluation of their compatibility would be akin to making an educated guess. In reality, the most accurate prediction we could make would simply be based on how similar partners are on attractiveness, educational background, and religious and political beliefs. This is why the science of matchmaking is still in its infancy: Love is hard to predict.

And yet people increasingly act as if they are true dating experts, especially when they are single. Have you ever tried online dating? Daters have never had a bigger choice of potential partners than now. For example, the website Plenty of Fish has more than five million users, and at any time you will find hundreds of thousands of people online, which should, at least in theory, represent paradise for those eager to customize their partners according to their wish list:

- Nonsmoker
- Liberal
- Christian
- At least five feet nine inches
- Lawyer or doctor
- Likes horror movies

You name it.

Online dating provides unprecedented technological scope for those who wish to apply a formulaic or mathematical approach to dating and long-term partner identification. Sadly, though, the method is no more effective than a chance encounter in a bar. To the horror of many, arranged marriages are more likely to result in relationship success than online dating relationships are. The implications are clear: Don't over-rationalize your choices, don't focus too much on your "shopping list," and embrace the unpredictable element of love.

As Victoria Elizabeth Coren, a columnist and former poker champion, noted, if we start by consistently demanding similarity in a potential partner, then all we can ever discover are the differences. There is something wonderful, even magical, about the beginning phase of any relationship when you slowly realize the similarities you share. Avoid calculating a shopping list of everything you want to see in your partner; go with the flow and embrace the surprises that come with falling in love.[8]

Don't Hope for Perfection → *Work on Improving*
What You Have

The world has around seven billion human inhabitants, give or take a few. The female-to-male sex ratio is roughly fifty-fifty, and 30 percent of the people of whichever sex you are interested in fall within your typical dating age range. This leaves you with a dating pool of just over one billion people.

I recall an old interview in which Jack Nicholson observed that on an average day he would meet more people than most do in their entire lifetimes (I think the number was one thousand). Even if you met as many people per day as Nicholson, it would take you twenty-eight hundred years to meet your entire dating pool. Or, if you wanted to find your perfect match in fifty years' time, you would need to meet around fifty-five thousand people a day. If you think relying on chance is a better alternative, you'd better be lucky! If there are one billion potential matches for you in the world, what is the probability that your "perfect match" visits your local mall, sits next to you on a long flight, or attends your high school reunion?

The perfect match illusion will not only keep you single for longer; it will threaten the success of your current relationship. Eli Finkel, a psychologist at Northwestern University and a dating scholar, recently observed that those who believe in romantic soul mates and that a relationship is either "meant to be" or not are more likely to quit their relationships when times get tough. On the other hand, those who believe in working through problems and growing their romantic relationships are more likely to overcome challenges, instead of simply giving up.[9]

And yet, the vast majority of people in Western civilization are inclined to believe they have a perfect match. For instance, more than seven in ten Americans[10] think there is an ideal soul mate for them somewhere. Whether they are currently dating that person or not, their belief is that there is just one perfect match for them, with everyone else being imperfect candidates. Although this view has romantic appeal, it is in stark contrast to the fact that one in two marriages in America now end in divorce. Even if you believe that you will be compatible with only 10 percent of the people in your potential dating pool, that implies that you have a hundred million good matches, so it is possible to remain optimistic without being delusional, or believing there is just one perfect candidate for you.

Avoid hoping for perfection and you will learn to appreciate what you have and work to make it even better. Every relationship has potential, but in order to make the most of it you need to work on it. Making what you have better is a much more feasible prospect than just bumping into someone who is a better match for you. To achieve this, you can simply start by focusing on small things: little changes, concrete activities, and behaviors that can be modified to result in a better, happier routine. Talking to your partner (or a potential partner) and agreeing on common goals is a good start; then reviewing the changes and discussing whether things have improved will help you achieve bigger goals, because you will build upon your initial accomplishments. The bottom line: Learn to be happy with what you have, and you will not be unhappy about what you don't. As Oscar Wilde once remarked, most people are made unhappy either by not getting what we want, or by getting it. In reality, there is no reason to be unhappy about either.

There's a Time to Fake Dating Confidence

Over the past several years, psychologists have been investigating the Michelangelo illusion, the psychological process by which lovers or daters bring out the best in each other. This phenomenon owes its name to the famous Italian artist Michelangelo Buonarroti, who regarded sculpting as the art of unleashing a perfect figure from a mere block of stone, which contained in it only potential. Dr. Madoka Kumashiro and colleagues conducted a series of psychological studies on daters and partners. They showed that, like Michelangelo's notion of sculpting, lovers tend to reveal the inner beauty of their partners, making them feel that they are becoming a better version of themselves.[11]

Thus, love, in part, is about finding someone who can help us reduce the perceived gap between who we are and who we want to be. A compatible partner can help you become the person you aspire to be, revealing and unleashing the best qualities you possess. If you haven't found that person yet, think about him or her as a sculptor searching for a stone. In sculpting, finding the right stone is an essential step of the process. In order to maximize the chances that you are the "stone of choice" for your sculptor, you will need to do your bit, which is where faking confidence is useful. Indeed, seeming confident to potential partners will help them see your potential, not least because if you don't come across as confident they will be more likely to pay attention to your insecurities and defects. Fake a moderate amount of self-love and you will entice others to explore and reveal your inner beauty. If you don't, you will alert others to your weaknesses, which should not be displayed until the sculpting process begins.

Finding a partner is similar to finding a job. You put yourself on the market, search for available opportunities, and show your best side to trigger others' interest. Jobs are based on a contract or agreement between an employer and an employee; every relationship has a contract or agreement between the two partners. As with a job, there are things that you can and cannot do, things that get you promoted and demoted (or fired), and there are specific roles and tasks for both partners.

When you go to a job interview, do you tell your potential employer all the negative things about yourself? No. This is not to say he or she believes you don't have any, but the point is that the revelation of negative aspects about you can be left until later. This applies to dating as well. Our social contract dictates that we show off our best side on a first date; if you are too open about your weaknesses, you will put people off. This may sound like unnecessary advice, but many people reveal too many of their problems on a first date. There is a time to tell the person you are trying to seduce that you are divorced, that you dislike his haircut, or that you have been unemployed for three years. The first date isn't it.

Not exposing your problems on a first date isn't enough; you need to be sure to exaggerate your strengths—people *expect* it. It is a bit like looking at a person's résumé. When recruiters do this, they assume that candidates have exaggerated their achievements by at least 20 percent. If they say they are fluent French speakers, it means they can string a few words in French or order food in a French restaurant. If a person says she has "basic" IT skills in an English-speaking country, it means she can switch on a computer, etc. Even if you don't fake it, people will still "discount" 20 percent from your reported accomplishments, whether on your résumé or on a first date. If you want them to get an accurate impression of how good you are, be sure to exaggerate a little. To put this into context, if on a first date you are talking about how sporty you are, you might tell your date that you love tennis, play often, and love keeping fit. In reality you may only play casually once a week with friends, but if you exaggerate the point a little, your date will probably walk away with the memory that you like sports, not that you are a fitness maniac. A little exaggeration of your skills makes it more likely that you'll impress your date and give him something to remember.

Faking a moderate amount of confidence will therefore ensure that those who find you attractive will find you even more attractive, and those who find you interesting will find you even more interesting. Here are four ways you can effectively fake confidence and entice others to become your personal Michelangelo.

1) Hide Your Insecurities

We do not succeed at anything by eliminating our weaknesses, but rather, by getting better at what we are already good at. There are two types of faults: those you can improve on and those you can't. The former can be fixed; it is the most common category. However, the more time you devote to trying to minimize your faults, the less time you will have to nurture your talents, maximize your strengths, and capitalize on your real assets. Faults, then, are pointless and harmless. There is something very uncharming about perfectionists who work too hard on minimizing their defects—they are mostly seen as obsessive and freaky by others, as the plastic surgery junkies in gossip magazines confirm. You might think you have personal faults such as being clumsy or overly impulsive, but these could be the very features that a potential partner would love about you. So, instead of trying to eradicate these faults, make a list—for each one you think you have, find a strength that makes up for it, and further develop it until you are proud of it. By doing this, you may find your-self more able to talk about yourself in a positive light when on a date, taking the focus off the negative features you believe you have. The people we date can find those out for themselves later! If you spend too much time trying to fix your weaknesses, chances are that you will develop an endless sense of insecurity, which will conta-giously turn into disliking other things about yourself and eventually result in there being little or nothing to admire in you. Conversely, the reverse strategy (developing and nurturing the strengths and tal-ents you already possess) will eliminate your weaknesses, because you and others will stop focusing on them.

2) Cultivate Your USPs

This builds on the previous point. The best salespeople are those capable of making anything attractive to others, but how? By identify-ing and highlighting its unique features and turning them into a unique selling point, or USP. As Don Draper, the fictional advertising genius and main character in *Mad Men*, asks before creating a new campaign for a product, "What's its benefit?" If you know the things that make you unique, you can turn them into something special.

Focusing on your strengths will help clarify what makes you different to everyone else. What's your USP? Is it your conversa-tional skill, your sense of humor, your kindness, a specific part of your body or face? Any trait has the potential to be the X factor so long as you have it and others don't, or if you have more of it than others do. Instead of copying others, then, you should be as differ-ent from them as possible. For example, Lady Gaga recognized that she had more of a wild flair for fashion and costume than other fe-male pop stars. She cultivated this as her USP and this is ultimately what makes her stand out. If you can identify something most people have in common but which you differ on then you ought to consider cultivating it and marketing it as much as you can because it could turn out to be a great USP. More important, if you are passionate about your USP you will be able to convey confidence to others, as you will come across as original and enthusiastic. And the best part of it is that you will not need to distort reality, either to others or to yourself.

3) Focus on Others

In order to fake confidence, it is important that you focus on others (which will in turn stop you from focusing too much on yourself). Remember our discussion about how to build social competence? The same applies to relationships. In a world where the majority of people are just too self-obsessed to pay attention to others, it is not a bad idea to be part of the minority. Talking about yourself will make others pay attention to you without necessarily attracting genuine interest, *and* you will risk looking like a narcissist. It will also make others compete with you for attention, in particular narcissists, who get quite aggressive in those situations. Don't go there. Instead, try to work out what other people are thinking, feeling, and doing. The more accurately you interpret what they want, the easier it will be for you to provide it. But in most cases, people will just want your attention, and if you give it to them they will see you as more likable, friendly, fun, interesting, *and* confident, not least because you will be too distracted to expose your insecurities. It is about finding the balance. While it is important to show off your USPs, it is not to suggest that the date become a live version of your personal ad. Being able to listen and give attention to your date while simultaneously being confident of your own USPs (and talking about them when the time is right) will make you come across in the most positive light.

Many of the seemingly most confident people I have ever met are masters of faking, and, as they've admitted in turn to me, all of them know that the trick is to focus on others rather than themselves. In fact, when you meet people who just talk about themselves and ignore other people's existence, they are either unsuccessfully faking confidence or simply deluded, which becomes clear as soon as you realize that their displays of confidence have no relationship to their actual competence. On the other hand, people who are genuinely confident also tend to focus on others, because they don't need to brag about their accomplishments or get other people's approval for their achievements.

Focusing on others, then, is the ultimate bluff, because it's not really a bluff at all—if you are genuinely modest and low-key, then use it to your benefit. In a sensible world, one would expect people who act modest to be perceived as being both less confident and less competent, but given that so many people in the world are deluded about their competence, we no longer tend to interpret displays of arrogance or showcasing as a sign of competence. People who are slightly unconfident allegedly want to avoid drawing attention from others, but, being self-obsessed, they end up spending most of their time talking about their own insecurities, forcing others to pay attention to them (they may achieve the same level of attention narcissists get, except they don't enjoy it as much). Who, then, has time to pay attention to others? People who are confident and secure. Focus on others and you will seem competent.

4) Flirt

There is arguably no better way to fake confidence than flirting. In fact, flirting will make others like you more, which will increase your competence and give you genuine confidence. Tons of scientific studies show that flirting creates reciprocal liking—that is, if you show interest in and attraction to others they will reciprocate by being interested in and attracted to you. In one of the first studies in this area, Joel Gold and his colleagues from the University of Maine set out to determine whether people increased their liking for a dissimilar person if they were persuaded that the person liked them or was interested in them.[12] To this end, they created a fake romantic situation by having an attractive female confederate chat with some of the male participants and fake interest in them by making eye contact and leaning on them. Despite her blatant physical displays of interest, the confederate disagreed with participants on a number of important topics of conversation. The same confederate also met with a second group of male participants, with whom she didn't flirt and instead just had minimal interaction. After interacting with the confederate, both groups of participants reported their level of liking for her as well as how similar they perceived her to be to them in terms of attitudes and values. As predicted, men who were subjected to the confederate's flirting showed higher levels of liking for her *and* perceived her values and beliefs as more similar to their own (despite the explicit disagreements during conversation) than the group of males who just had minimal interaction with her.

The reciprocal liking effect has since been replicated in hundreds of psychological studies. In fact, out of all the factors that determine whether someone likes you or not, one of the strongest—if not *the* strongest—is whether that person thinks you like him. And it works in both directions: When someone is marginally interested in you but finds out that you don't like him, he will be less interested in you. Flirting is *the* most effective way to get others to like you, which means that if you flirt you will not just seem more confident in the dating game but will also improve your actual success rate. In fact, seeming confident is only the second best outcome you will achieve by flirting—the first is to actually seduce people. That is, if your flirting is effective (in the traditional sense), people will be seduced whether they see you as confident or not. If, on the other hand, your flirting is ineffective, you will at least come across as confident.

In short, there's a lot you can do to boost your dating competence. Part of the process depends on making better decisions, and your strategy can improve if you start aiming higher or lower than you have been, avoid being overly rational, and ditch your unrealistic expectations of finding a "perfect" match. All this is part of the preparation process, which will boost your performance once you are interacting with potential romantic partners. Hiding your insecurities, highlighting your USPs, focusing on others, and flirting will make those interactions even more successful. Thus you gotta gain some competence in order to fake confidence in order to gain more competence.

Using It:

• Work on developing an accurate perception of your own eligibility.
  —You could ask those closest to you, even previous partners, for their opinions of your eligibility.

- Don't aim too high when choosing a partner.
  —Keep your expectations realistic by monitoring how picky you are being.
  —Give potential partners a chance to impress you before dismissing them.

- Don't aim too low when choosing a partner.
  —Work on your confidence with being single and make sure to enjoy time on your own.
  —Avoid dating people who you know are not good matches.
  —Seek advice and opinions from those who know you best; they are likely to give you some honest feedback on whom you are dating.

- Try not to over-rationalize the dating process.
  —Don't calculate and demand similarity from the outset of a new relationship; be patient and see what happens.

- Work on improving what you have rather than hoping for continual perfection.
  —Focus on working hard in a relationship instead of obsessing about the idea of a soul mate.
  —Seek professional help and tackle challenges head-on instead of assuming that it just isn't "meant to be."
  —Keep the communication up with your partner to ensure you are both on the same page.

- Learn **when** and **how** to fake dating confidence.
  —Hide your insecurities on a first date. Make a list of your strengths and strategize on how you can foster them before the date.

—Cultivate your own USPs: take some time to think about this. Seek advice and opinions from those closest to you.

—Focus on others: when starting to date someone, don't talk about yourself too much.

- Flirt—make an obvious effort to take an interest in a potential partner. Make eye contact and body contact where appropriate.

7

A Healthier Life

The greatest of follies is to sacrifice health for any other kind of happiness.

—Arthur Schopenhauer (1788–1860)

Your Well-being Is in Your Hands

When it comes to health, especially serious health issues, it is clear that a person's goal should be to become more competent rather than more confident. But what does health competence even mean?

In the view of medical doctors, health competence is the absence of disease or disability. Yet, many people live happy lives while coping with chronic health problems or severe medical conditions.[1] Moreover, because humans are now living longer than ever before, a growing number of people are able to cope with illnesses that were once deadly. The implication is that physical disease does not necessarily threaten our overall well-being—our ability to feel content with our general existence and life satisfaction.

On the other hand, when we take into account how people *feel* about their health and well-being—what psychologists call "subjective well-being"—there is a clear discrepancy between objective and subjective health indicators. For example, Dr. William Strawbridge and colleagues classified older people as unhealthy if they exhibited known medical conditions or signs of mental decline, or were not actively engaged in society.[2] According to these stricter criteria (you had to show absence of the three in order to be deemed healthy), 81 percent of their sample was ill, yet more than 50 percent of the participants saw themselves as healthy. The bottom line is that there is only marginal overlap between people's self-perceived and actual health in the overall population: Health confidence ain't competence.

As two leading health psychologists recently noted, there is a large amount of subjectivity regarding the notion of health. One person might seek medical help when she experiences muscle pain or mild nausea, while another person may consider these to be fairly average aspects of normal life.[3] In fact, most of the things that make us feel good are bad for our health: Sugar, alcohol, caffeine, fat, and spending our weekends as couch potatoes are all more comforting and subjectively rewarding than their healthier alternatives.

Many psychologists regard health as a sort of IQ test, and they have a point. In order to be healthy you need to solve certain problems, fulfill certain tasks, and avoid some activities. For example, being healthy requires you to understand the impact of different types of food and drinks, as well as the value of physical exercise. It is also important to correctly interpret symptoms and take appropriate measures once they are identified. Moreover, in order to be healthy you ought to realize that certain behaviors carry important health threats. Sometimes, information is unreliable or unavailable— for example, it took a few decades for experts to determine how harmful the effects of smoking cigarettes are, and every known diet has as many endorsers as critics. However, at any point in time, people who make better use of the available health knowledge have

an advantage over those who don't, which means that they should
be better able to solve the practical problem of gaining and maintaining health. You could stay informed about current progress in
health and medicine using various websites or even just keep up
with regular checkups with your doctor to ensure you are following
their latest advice for healthy living.

In that sense, we can see not only how health is a form of competence but also that the capacity to obtain and maintain health is
in itself a type of competence: Some people are more health savvy
than others, which enables them to also be healthier. Actually increasing your own health competence involves working on increasing your health IQ. So read, learn, and seek advice. This might even
mean trying out different things—new exercises or a different eating lifestyle—and then seeing which works for you and gets you in
the best shape. Health competence is about using the knowledge
that is out there and applying it to your own life in the optimal way.
Although it might require a great deal of practice, including some
experimentation and trial and error, as with any other domain of
competence, those who perform best tend to also work the hardest.
For example, health-conscious people pay close attention to their
dietary habits and monitor their fat, calories, and carb consumption
very carefully; they also tend to exercise regularly and they exert a
significant level of effort and self-control to resist unhealthy habits
such as overeating, drinking, smoking, and caffeine consumption.
In short, there is no big secret to being healthy; it is a well-defined
science rather than an art, and anybody has the capacity to improve
his or her health. Where we differ substantially is in our tendency
to put that capability into practice.

So what role does confidence play here? The common belief is
that a positive mind-set creates good health, but the only scientific

evidence in support of this is the finding that optimistic people are *slightly* more likely to persist in the face of difficulties.[4] For example, research has shown that people with an optimistic mind-set tend to recover faster from surgery and have lower illness and mortality rates.[5] However, many of those studies fail to account for previous health competence, and there is not much evidence of positive effects of optimism on objective health outcomes.[6] As Drs. Margaret Kern and Howard Friedman point out in their excellent review of the topic, no real evidence exists to support the claim that a positive mind-set can actually succeed in shrinking tumors or unclogging arteries.[7] In fact, it is often more adaptive to be *less* rather than more persistent, not least because not everything we persist in can be attained, and not everything we pursue *should* be attained (more on this later).

As in any domain of competence, the correlation between confidence and health competence is at best ambiguous and at worst meaningless, casting serious doubt on the clichéd idea that higher confidence promotes better health. It is ambiguous because it is hardly ever a sign of a causal link between confidence and competence—people may feel insecure about their health as a consequence of actual health symptoms, and the same is true for those who feel confidence about their health status. And it is meaningless because for most people there is not much relation between their perceived and actual health states; in other words, most people are generally quite inept at assessing their own health (especially when their assessments are positive). Furthermore, a large number of scientific studies indicate that higher confidence can have disastrous health consequences: Most of the well-documented health-threatening behaviors—drinking, overeating, smoking, drug consumption—would not be so prevalent if people felt less immune to their adverse effects, and that immunity is fueled by an inappropriately high self-confidence. In fact, the main take-home message from this chapter is that low confidence leads to better health than high confidence does, and that the only beneficial type of high confidence is the one produced by genuine gains in health competence. However, when confidence is high as a result of self-serving biases (which is sadly rather common), it can be quite unhealthy.

The Unhealthy Side of High Confidence

There is no better demonstration of the detrimental effects of high confidence than its negative effects on health. In this sense, high confidence is not assumed to mean the same thing as having an optimistic outlook on life. In regard to health, being highly confident relates to the security you feel about the state of your health and your indestructibility. Although there are hundreds of studies in this area, the great bulk of destructive health effects are a function of three counterproductive qualities of higher confidence:

- An inappropriate sense of immunity, which leads to higher and more frequent risk taking

- A sense of denial or poor self-awareness, which results from an obsession with maintaining a positive self-image and seeing oneself as "healthy" when one is not

- A false feeling of hope that persists even in the face of negative results; this perpetuates ineffective health behaviors

Let's discuss these points in more detail.

1. High Confidence Increases Risk Taking

Can higher confidence really worsen your health? Absolutely. Psychologist Peter Fischer, at the University of Graz (Austria), includes in his definition of risk-taking behavior its association with the potential to harm yourself through unhealthy life choices like smoking or by dangerous driving such as street racing. Higher confidence distorts your perception of risk and its consequences, creating a false sense of security and the illusion of immunity. In the United States, to name just one country, risky behaviors are now the leading cause of deadly injuries in children, adolescents, and young adults.[8] Take a look at these shocking statistics, all of which result from inflated confidence:

- Risk-taking behaviors such as alcohol consumption, speeding, and drug use have caused many of the traffic accidents that are responsible for up to 10 percent of fatalities in people between the ages of 10 and 24 worldwide. In the USA, roughly 5,000 individuals under the age of 21 die every year due to alcohol abuse and associated risk taking while driving.[9]

- The United States reported an estimate of 18.9 million new sexually transmitted disease cases in the year 2000. Forty-eight percent of these were among 15- to 24-year-olds and believed to be due to their risky sexual practices.

- Risky health behaviors such as smoking and binge drinking (i.e., consuming more than five alcohol units) are becoming more and more common in Western countries. Between 2002 and 2009, Germany saw the number of

15- to 19-year-old individuals treated for alcohol abuse double.

The reason why higher confidence is a main cause of risk is that it eclipses fear. When you feel confident, you tend to consider negative outcomes as improbable or even rule them out completely, undermining real risks and failing to consider genuine threats. Risk can range from extreme risk aversion to extreme risk taking, and your confidence level determines where you stand on this continuum. Fear, perceived threats, anxiety, and caution are all big enemies of high confidence, which relates to fearless experimentation, sensation seeking, and danger.

Consider the case of cigarette smoking, which, even today, carries a higher death risk than all other common unhealthy activities put together.[10] Although you often hear smokers say that puffing gives them confidence (code for "relaxes me"), most people would not even start smoking if they felt less immune to the dangers involved. People often pick up smoking as a way to feel—or at least seem—more confident in social situations. This increase in their confidence level reduces the probability that these smokers will be deterred by the inherent risks of smoking and leads them to think that they will be able to give up easily whenever they decide. In line, introverts, who tend to be less confident than extroverts, have been found to smoke less[11] and to give up more easily than extroverts.[12]

Higher confidence fosters experimentation not only with cigarettes, but with most health-threatening substances, such as alcohol and illicit drugs. In a thorough review of the negative consequences of self-esteem, the most generic measure of confidence, British psychologist Nick Emler concluded that high self-esteem leads to greater willingness to take physical risks, which explains why people with higher self-esteem are more frequent alcohol and drug users despite being more satisfied with their lives.[13] For instance, surveys of college students found that higher self-esteem leads to greater willingness to drink.[14]

The detrimental effects of high confidence on health are not found merely at extreme levels of risk or high confidence. Given the pervasiveness of self-delusional biases, most people think that they are less susceptible to health problems, especially serious illnesses, than they actually are.[15] Paradoxically, then, the more confident you are about your health, the more likely you will be to ruin it. This type of paradox is known as a "self-defeating prophecy." Imagine a scenario in which two people of similar health visit a fortune-teller to inquire about their life expectancy. One of them is told that he will endure numerous health problems and is therefore likely to die young; the other, that he will live many years with no risk of any major illness. As a result of these prophecies, both men decide to alter their lifestyles—one to avoid dying young, the other to enjoy his predicted longevity. So the pessimistic forecast drives the first person to be healthier, while the optimistic forecast drives the second person to indulge in more risk-taking behaviors and an unhealthy lifestyle. In the end, the man with the pessimistic forecast ends up outliving the one with the optimistic forecast, and both forecasts are proven wrong.

Sadly, most people behave as if they have been given an optimistic forecast about their health. In what is arguably the most impressive longitudinal study relating to confidence and health, Dr. Howard Friedman and colleagues inspected the association between the personality characteristics of fifteen hundred eleven-year-old children and health outcomes seven decades later. They found that at any given age, optimistic and confident children were at higher risk of dying than their more pessimistic and unconfident counterparts, and the reason was their higher propensity to take health risks. In line, Dr. Friedman concluded that the key recipe to extend life is a combination of prudence and persistence: "The best childhood personality predictor of longevity was conscientiousness."[16]

Consider Ryan Dunn as an example: a young male daredevil and star of the TV series *Jackass*, who was killed in a horrific high-speed car crash in 2011 at the age of thirty-four. This is a prime example of someone who lived life taking extreme risks and, arguably, was overconfident to the extent that he believed he could drive at incredibly high speeds while under the influence of alcohol on the night of his accident. Tragically however, this risky behavior is what ultimately led to his early demise.

Another robust longitudinal study examined the effects of initial self-esteem on subsequent sexual behavior in a sample of more than eleven hundred participants. This impressive dataset tracked participants from the age of three until twenty-one. Females with higher self-esteem at age eleven were significantly more likely than those with lower self-esteem to be sexually initiated by the age of fifteen. Self-esteem was the only socially desirable predictor of early sexual activity; the other variables were all undesirable—school problems, early smoking, etc.[17] The explanation? Simple: Higher confidence led females to discount the health risks of premature sex. In line, another study reported that more confident women tended to dismiss the risk of pregnancy, and even when they were reminded of the risks, they believed that such misfortunes wouldn't apply to them.[18] Have you ever watched the MTV show *16 and Pregnant*? Nearly every pregnant young woman on the program admits she did not use protection because she "just didn't think it would happen" to her. This explains the seemingly irrational finding that confident women who are sexually active think they are less likely to end up being pregnant than sexually inactive women.[19]

2. High Confidence Distorts Health Self-Views

The second health danger brought about by high confidence is denial, and self-deception that involves convincing yourself that you're healthy when you're not. This can lead to ignorance of warnings or refusal to get treatment or change a behavior, because you think you aren't at risk. This is one of the reasons for the ineffectiveness of health campaigns that rely on threats. For instance, even if smokers are presented with huge warning signs, such as SMOKING KILLS or SMOKING CAUSES LUNG CANCER, they will rarely see themselves as the targets of those messages.

How many smokers, drinkers, or drug users are willing to acknowledge that they have an addiction? Very few. The reason is obvious: Acknowledging their addiction would make them feel stupid, because it would force them to accept that they are doing something stupid *to themselves*. A much more bearable alternative, especially if the goal is to keep smoking, drinking, or getting high, is to pretend (fool yourself into thinking) that nothing is wrong. Remember Richard Feynman's words? "You are the easiest person to fool." The main problem with fooling yourself is that it makes you incapable of telling the truth even if you want to. When you fool yourself, you are neither telling the truth nor lying to others. When people say, "I am not in denial," they usually are but just don't know it; it's an essential feature of being in denial.

The psychological mechanism that causes people to deny unhealthy or undesirable habits is known as "cognitive dissonance." Humans are, perhaps surprisingly, rational creatures and feel the need to perceive a harmony between their beliefs and behavior. When they don't, they experience unpleasant feelings of incoherence, confusion, and annoyance—this is cognitive dissonance, and it forces people to reconsider their self-views. In other words, cognitive dissonance points out that we have a distorted view of ourselves, and one of the ways to avoid experiencing dissonance is to distort reality. Ironically, then, our quest for rationality ends up making us irrational. For example, if smokers accepted the fact that smoking is deadly, they would feel stupid whenever they smoke; if drinkers accepted the fact that they have a drinking problem, they would feel stupid whenever they drink, and so on. Leon Festinger, the social psychologist who pioneered cognitive dissonance research in America fifty years ago, noted that since the act of smoking is incompatible with knowledge that smoking is harmful, smokers are motivated to distort their beliefs about smoking in order to minimize the experience of dissonance (and keep smoking). Unsurprisingly, the more people smoke, the more they deny that smoking is bad.[20] Delusions are the fuel that keeps addictions going.

Cognitive dissonance does not just affect smoking or health-related behaviors—we all experience it. For instance, dissonance is the reason you decide to stop being friends with people after they disagree with you on important values; or why you force yourself to believe that an expensive meal tasted good, or that a long, arduous journey was worthwhile. Facing the facts would be more painful and harm your self-esteem. Indeed, one of the most compelling findings in the whole of psychology is that people's attempts to avoid cognitive dissonance are by and large the result of their uncompromising desire to maintain a positive self-view, to the degree of distorting reality even on fairly mundane matters. In one of the earliest experiments on this, Jack Brehm asked subjects to indicate how much they liked different household appliances (e.g., fridges, washing machines, ovens). After providing their ratings, subjects were asked to pick one of the appliances to receive as a gift, but there was a caveat: They could only pick from two appliances they had rated equally. As cognitive dissonance theory predicts, participants increased their liking for the appliance they picked as a gift, rating it as more attractive than they initially had.[21]

Given that dissonance reduction is driven by the need to maintain a positive self-image, one would expect confident people to be more motivated to avoid cognitive dissonance. This hypothesis was tested in a couple of elegant experiments designed by Hart Blanton and colleagues. Their first study recruited participants for a blind tasting of Coke versus Pepsi. Before this task, participants reported how much they preferred one drink over the other. As you have probably noticed, most regular cola drinkers claim that they can easily tell the difference between Coke and Pepsi, especially given that they tend to have a well-defined preference for one of the two drinks. However, if there is one thing you should have learned from reading this book by now, it's that there's a big difference between what people think they can do (their confidence) and what they actually can do (their competence). Accordingly, the experiment showed that participants overestimated their ability to distinguish between the two colas, especially when they reported stronger preference for one of the two. The more expertise participants thought they possessed, the more they were "forced" to display confidence in their judgments in order to eliminate the cognitive dissonance—even when they were wrong. As the researchers observed, the "association between perceived preference and judgment confidence reflected a self-protective motive. As preference increased, the motivation to believe in the veracity of one's judgment also increased."[22] Thus participants who felt knowledgeable and important were less able to realize that they were incompetent, because their desire to feel competent blinded their willingness to accept that they were wrong, so they ended up faking confidence to themselves.

Dr. Blanton and colleagues set out to replicate the results from the first experiment in a high-stakes setting, namely college students taking an exam. The researchers used the occasion to test whether students who were more concerned about maintaining a positive self-view were more prone to distort their beliefs about the exam in order to avoid experiencing dissonance. Before the exam, students were asked to report how important it was for them to do well on that assignment. After the exam, students indicated how confident they were that they had performed well on the test, but there was a caveat: A random group of students were told that if they did poorly on the test their grade wouldn't count; the other students were not told anything, so they assumed that their performance on the exam would affect their final grade. As Dr. Blanton and colleagues predicted, the more students cared about the exam, the more confident they were about their performance, even after adjusting for their actual performance. However, for the group that was told that they were allowed to drop the grade if they did not do well, there was no significant relationship between the degree to which they cared about the test and their confidence in their performance.

These results indicate that higher confidence is an unconscious strategy to minimize the experience of health-related dissonance, which explains why confident people are more likely to take health risks even after they are presented with clear information about those risks. Put differently, there is a tension between maintaining high health confidence (perceiving yourself as healthy) and accurate self-awareness (realizing that you are unhealthy). However, confidence ends up not only eclipsing self-awareness but also perpetuating the behaviors that threaten your health. Imagine a smoker who is made aware of his unhealthy habits and, for a minute, feels uncomfortable about it, but then decides to simply ignore that assertion and tells himself, "There is nothing to worry about; you are fine." Clearly, such a reaction would perpetuate his smoking. Thus, confidence acts as a psychological shield or resistance against reality checks, keeping our conscience clean even when we are clearly damaging our health.

James Jaccard, Tonya Dodge, and Vincent Guilamo-Ramos conducted a longitudinal study to investigate the role of confidence underlying risky sexual behaviors in adolescents.[23] Their results revealed that the more confident participants were about their knowledge of contraception, the more likely they were to be pregnant in the future. There are two explanations for these findings: first, the low connection between confidence (their perceived knowledge) and competence (how much they really knew); second, the fact that people's confidence in their knowledge inflated their perceived ability to have sex without negative consequences. In other words, people's desire to feel competent led them to maintain fake perceptions of knowledge, which in turn maximized their exposure to risk. As Blanton and his team at the University at Albany noted: "Accurate knowledge provides many rewards, chief among these being increased abilities to predict, control, and respond to the social world. Feeling confident in the accuracy of one's beliefs and judgments should thus foster a sense of security in the face of both mundane and important decisions. Unfortunately, the comfort gained through such confidence is often unwarranted."[24] People with high confidence "tend to minimize their own vulnerability. They employ a variety of cognitive strategies to convince themselves that bad things will not or cannot happen to them, and ignore disagreeable information. Thus, they distance themselves from the potentially harmful consequences of risky behavior."[25] In the famous words of the French philosopher Voltaire: "Doubt is not a pleasant condition, but certainty is absurd."[26]

These findings indicate that unrealistic high confidence is a defensive strategy to avoid facing the fact that one is less competent than one thinks. Higher confidence distorts how people perceive their health and health-related behavior. Given that humans have limited mental energy to pursue their goals, including health-related aims, any energy employed in maintaining high self-views is wasted. This waste creates a disruption of one's goal fulfillment, known as "ego depletion," whereby mental energy needed for self-improvement (changes in competence) is pointlessly allocated to maintaining high self-views (boosting confidence). This is why confident people react more defensively and aggressively when criticized,[27] and why they stubbornly attempt to maintain their high self-views when they feel threatened.[28] Conversely, coming to terms with your negative self-views will make you less defensive to criticism (you already know what others tell you and you agree with them), and it therefore opens the door to self-improvement. If you are in a situation in which your health is poor and you know it, what you want is to improve your health. If you are in a situation in which you are trying to feel good about your health, what you want is reassurance—you want to be certain about your self-views, and you neglect your actual health.

And here are some of the significant health implications:

- Confident people tend to think they are better at following healthy lifestyles than they actually are. For instance, optimists have much higher confidence in their ability to lose weight even when they don't lose any actual weight.[29]

- Confident smokers are more threatened (than unconfident smokers) by exposure to facts about the harmful effects of smoking, because it makes it much harder for
  them to accept the idea of doing something stupid.[30]

- Confident adolescents think their parents approve of
  their drinking habits, whereas less confident adolescents
  are aware that they don't.[31]

- Confident college students are a lot more likely to binge-
  drink, smoke, be sleep deprived, and have multiple sexual partners than their less confident counterparts.[32]

In brief, self-serving biases fueled by high confidence conspire
against people's health. These biases make confident people more
likely to drink, take drugs, and have unprotected sex, and they also
generate false self-improvement expectations.

3. High Confidence Creates False Health Hopes

It would be good if the destructive health effects of high confidence only applied to a minority of people—i.e., those with inflated
self-views or optimistic biases. Unfortunately, they are the norm, at
least when it comes to common health problems. While the poor of
this world get sick and die young because of lack of resources, people with resources incur most health issues from making unrealistic
evaluations of their problems. "In denial" is a term that is commonly
applied to most of the people who fall victim to addiction and fail to
acknowledge that they cannot control their self-destructive behavior. In that sense, their minds replicate many of the psychological
characteristics found in overconfident people, whether they are

addicts or not. Yet if we were more realistic about our slim chances of winning the fight against addiction and successfully changing unhealthy habits, we would actually attain much higher success rates, and perhaps never have these destructive habits in the first place. In other words, less confidence would lead to more competence.

Take a few minutes to reflect on these facts:

- Most people are unrealistic about their chances of achieving health goals and judge their goals as easier to attain than they actually are.[33]

- Most diets achieve short-term success at best.[34]

- People discharged from alcohol abuse programs tend to be unrealistically optimistic and relapse shortly thereafter.[35] For example, 90 percent of treated alcoholics have at least one drink in the three months post-treatment, and one in two return to pretreatment levels of drinking in the next twelve months.[36]

- Smokers underestimate how hard it is to give up: More than 50 percent of adolescents and almost as many adults believe that they are able to just "smoke for a few years and then quit."[37] The reality? Even after repeated attempts, only 10 percent of smokers remain abstinent six to twelve months after giving up.[38] For instance, of the thirty million Americans who quit smoking in the 1980s, 80 percent did not manage to abstain for more than one year.[39] Smokers who think they can give up smoking while also quitting other unhealthy habits (e.g., binge eating or drinking) are even more likely to fail.[40]

- The small number of people who succeed at quitting addictions or changing important health habits do so only after the fifth attempt.[41]

- Because most people have unrealistic expectations about the impact that fixing specific health issues will have on their lives, they will tend to be disappointed even when they achieve their goals. For example, research has shown that many dieters operate under the assumption that losing weight will somehow transform them into better human beings.[42] Therefore, successful dieters will often end up distorting reality to accommodate such expectations. For instance, people who decide to exercise more frequently often end up believing that they are taller than they were before committing to exercise.[43]

In the face of such prevalent failure rates, it is no doubt illogical that so many people remain optimistic and confident about their ability to improve their health. Dr. Janet Polivy, a renowned health psychologist, refers to this phenomenon as the "false hope syndrome"; that is, the cycle of failure, inadequate interpretation of reality, and continued efforts to renew the quest for health even after repeated failure and with an improbable success rate.[44] This does not mean that you cannot improve your health status. However, being aware of the low probability of achieving this will actually make you more successful, while the more confident you are about accomplishing difficult tasks, the more likely it is that you will fail.

Dr. Polivy explains that people begin by setting themselves difficult (sometimes impossible) challenges in order to change. Many are aiming to kick unwanted (albeit intrinsically rewarding) behaviors to the curb. Ultimately, we fail to achieve these difficult tasks but continue to believe that with a few adjustments, success is still a possibility. Those of us who try ludicrous, extreme diets are often the worst culprits. If we actually set more realistic goals to start with, we might be more successful. But this would clash with people's "personal agenda," says Dr. Polivy. Adjusting a diet such that it means losing less weight, takes longer to see results, and consequently causes people to abandon their dreams of a total social and personal makeover is not what these people are willing to do. Diets advertise big promises in order to attract customers. It is the very size of these promises that means people cannot fulfill them. So they will just keep going back! [45] The key implication of the false hope syndrome is that people would be more successful at fixing their health problems if they were *less* confident in their ability to attain their goals, but since that requires coming to terms with a less favorable self-view, most people prefer to remain delusional.

The Healthy Side of Lower Confidence

Whereas high confidence can harm your health to the point of being lethal, low confidence is an important driver of health competence. Remember the evolutionary role of anxiety? Low confidence is an adaptive tool that evolved to protect us from danger and threats. At an extreme level, it is manifested physically and emotionally in the form of intense anxiety, which stops us from doing something stupid and helps us escape threats. To our evolutionary ancestors, anxiety was a life-saving signal to help them overcome dangerous situations.

When anxiety causes low confidence, it is sending a message to prevent us from damaging our health. When we fail at it, in particular after repeated experiences of anxiety or in the face of important losses, we still have one protective resource in our repertoire: depression (remember our discussion about the adaptive evolutionary meaning of depression). Indeed, the point of depression is to force us to accept blame, face the facts, and avoid similar disappointments in the future. Thus humans evolved anxiety and depression as highly adaptive competencies to face difficult challenges, especially those requiring high levels of dedication. If fever is our body's attempt to coordinate a response to an infection, anxiety is our mind's attempt to cope with stress, and depression is its attempt to deal with taxing ideas—the loss of someone we love, or coming to terms with failure.[46] Most notably, depression stops us from wasting time on unattainable goals, reducing the probability of experiencing false hope.

If all this sounds too gloomy, that's because you have habituated to hearing unrealistic optimistic messages, such as "Don't ever give up, no matter what happens," or "Ignore failure, stay positive, and you will succeed." If you manage to avoid wasting precious energy on tasks that are extremely hard to accomplish, you will free up valuable energy and resources to devote to more attainable goals. Being aware of how difficult goals are eliminates the need to self-enhance or distort reality when we fail to achieve them. The ability to know when to give up is just as important as knowing when to try harder.[47]

More important, successful self-change requires accepting responsibility for one's state, even if the cost is depression. In line, studies have found that smokers who blame themselves are more likely to quit smoking,[48] and that if dieters blamed themselves more they would attain higher success rates losing weight,[49] which is why autonomous dieters do better than those who put their hopes in a program or a coach. As Carl Jung, one of the founders of psycho-

analysis, wisely remarked: "Man needs difficulties; they are necessary for health."

Low Confidence Extends Life

Let us now look at the positive health effects of low confidence from
a purely pragmatic perspective. No more evolutionary theory or biology; just sheer facts. Low confidence protects you from health problems by motivating you to seek advice and minimizing risk taking.
In other words, low confidence extends life.

A nifty study by Francesca Gino and her colleagues at Harvard
and the University of Pennsylvania highlights the importance of low
confidence as a determinant of people's willingness to seek advice.[50]
In a series of ingenious experiments, the researchers manipulated
participants' anxiety levels (e.g., by showing some of the subjects
videos of extreme sports or scary accidents) to demonstrate that
those who experienced higher anxiety were more likely to seek and
pay attention to advice from others on a subsequent decision-making
task. The authors also measured the impact of anxiety on participants' confidence, and their results showed that higher anxiety increased willingness to seek advice on the decision-making task
because it lowered people's confidence in their ability to do well. In
other words, when anxious people don't differ in confidence, they
are equally likely to seek advice; but when they do, lower confidence
increases the propensity to seek and pay attention to advice.

Howard Friedman refers to this phenomenon as "healthy neu-
roticism"; he observes that insecurity "may lead to reports of lower
well-being, more psychosomatic symptoms, and more doctor's visits,
[which] objectively lead to fewer diseases and longer life." In their

longitudinal analyses of the fifteen hundred children who were followed up until they were eighty years old, Dr. Friedman and colleagues
found that less confident men had lower mortality risk, indicating
that low confidence is an important antidote to men's natural risk-
taking tendencies. In fact, few trends are as conclusive as the sex
difference in health-related risks and mortality. Check out the following stats for the United States:[51]

- Women live longer than men despite suffering from similar or even higher frequency of illness (morbidity).

- Women are at least 50 percent more likely than men to
  visit the doctor—for example, in 2005, 45 percent of
  men made preventive visits to the doctor, compared to 75
  percent of women.

- Around 15 percent more men than women are regular
  alcohol consumers.

- Although heavy drinking rates are similar for both sexes
  (around 5 percent of adults), the incidence of "light"
  drinking is 30 percent for men versus 7 percent for
  women, while the incidence of "moderate" drinking is 22
  percent for men versus just 4 percent for women.

- Alcohol-related deaths are 3 times higher in men than in
  women.

- Although the gap is narrowing, there are about 5 percent
  more male than female smokers—in addition, 12 percent
  more women than men have never smoked.

- Ten percent more men than women are likely to use illicit
  drugs at some point in their lives.

- Men are also about 10 percent more frequent users of recreational drugs (e.g., cannabis, cocaine, and ecstasy).

- Approximately 10 percent more men are overweight than women.

Unsurprisingly, men have higher death rates for twelve of the fifteen leading mortality causes in the United States, and they die an average of five years earlier than women. The two underlying reasons, namely higher risk taking and lower prevention, can be attributed to men's higher confidence. As noted by Dr. Ruben Pinkhasov of the Maimonides Medical Center in New York, who reported the preceding statistics:[52] "Men's importance on self-reliance, physical toughness, and emotional control all play in to their masculinity and inhibit their willingness to seek help from health professionals."

Or, if you prefer, women's lower confidence drives them to seek advice and minimize risks compared to men. Some men live longer than women, but mostly when they are less confident than typical men. By the same token, some women die younger than men, but partly because they take similar health risks and neglect preventive behaviors as most men do. What matters, then, is not sex, but confidence.

Earning Confidence (Through Well-being)

As the reviewed evidence suggests, health is just like any other area of competence in that (a) people tend to have a poor understanding of it; (b) the more confident people are, the more deluded they are about their health; and (c) less confident people are more realistic and likely to accept responsibility about their health problems. Yet, because health is more objective than other types of competence, which tend to depend more on what other people (but not necessarily doctors) think, lower confidence is even more important for attaining health than any other type of competence. Now, given that you are reading this book—and that you managed to get to this point—I doubt that you are the kind of person who needs to lower your confidence, but if you want to do that in relation to health, just spend some time reading up on health-related issues and speak to two or three friends whom you may consider health freaks to find out how hard they work to be where they are, and to get their views on how healthy you are. As a rule of thumb, we should always compare ourselves with people who are much better than we are—it may lower our confidence, but it will also incentivize us to be better than our peers. You can only get better if you aim higher.

This is the perfect moment to make a realistic assessment of your health situation. Perhaps you find yourself in need of improvement in one or many areas. Recognizing this is the key step to getting better. Allow this knowledge to motivate you—so, what are you waiting for?

Let me share with you the best case study for the positive power of low confidence as driver of health and well-being that I've ever come across: *The Biggest Loser* reality TV show. I profiled, coached, and followed up with the contestants in the UK edition for a couple of years. If you're not familiar, the show invites morbidly obese adults to spend eight weeks in a boot camp–style program in which they undergo an extreme fitness and dieting regimen.[53] Most of them have been seriously overweight or obese for more than a decade, which resulted in rock-bottom confidence and self-esteem levels. In fact, their obesity affected every other domain of competence:

romantic relationships (especially sex), social life, career success, and of course health, in many cases shortening their life expectancy by more than ten years.

And yet, *The Biggest Loser* contestants had one big advantage over the average person in the normal population, namely the fact that they admitted to having a problem and that they were the main cause of that problem. Contrast that with the vast majority of people who are in denial about their role and responsibility—for example, smokers who call themselves "social smokers," drug addicts who see themselves as "recreational users," or food addicts who blame their weight problems on their "slow metabolism" or "busy lifestyle." I'm sure you get the point.

Let's now hear from Kevin, the 2012 *Biggest Loser* winner and the heaviest contestant in the show's history (he was 450 pounds when I interviewed him for the show):[54]

Before taking part in *The Biggest Loser* my confidence and self-esteem were at rock bottom. My life was a constant of inner conversations that battered my own confidence and self-esteem. My self-talk was constantly negative about my health and appearance, and even the things I would say to my partner would involve some sort of self-abuse.

It was only once I had lost a significant amount of weight on the show and was back "in the real world" that I really started to notice how my confidence was growing. I felt better about myself daily, and each week when I got weighed and I had lost weight or each time I was wearing smaller clothes it was like a shot in the arm of self-esteem and confidence. At times I do feel my confidence slip back to my old ways, but I literally just pull my shoulders and chest up and out and walk like a man with confidence, and my newfound confidence comes back quickly.[55]

Kevin's journey was crowned by winning the competition and losing almost two hundred pounds in four months, but each of the contestants went through exactly the same process. They all started with rock-bottom confidence levels but were so eager to lose weight that their confidence didn't matter. They were all determined to work hard to achieve a monumental goal, and as soon as they started to make progress they became a bit more confident, which motivated them to work even harder. They all ended up winning, because they exceeded their weight loss target and recovered not just their confidence but also their health.

Kevin is the poster boy for what this book postulates, namely that your low confidence is there to protect you and motivate you to gain competence. Most people are so fixated on feeling confident that they are in denial, if not delusional, about their actual competence. What Kevin and the other *Biggest Loser* contestants show, however, is that lower confidence is a blessing.

Thus, low confidence causes high competence, which in turn causes realistic high confidence.

Conversely, high confidence causes low competence, which in turn causes denial, until one faces the facts and confidence is lowered—then, progress may start. When competence gains translate into confidence gains, they have long-standing positive effects on people's well-being and happiness. For instance, changing to a physically active lifestyle increases emotional well-being, energy levels, and self-confidence,[56] and physical exercise improves not only your health but also your self-views and confidence.[57] The implication is that earned confidence—that is, confidence based on real competence attainment—breeds future success, whereas delusional, unrealistic, self-enhanced confidence predicts future failure.[58]

Using It:

- Improve your health IQ.
  - —Read, learn, and seek advice. Gather information and try out different ways of healthy living.
  - —Stay health savvy: buy regular health magazines, keep a list of your goals and targets, and maintain checkups with your doctor. Stay informed about new developments.
  - —Practice makes perfect! You are going to have to really work at improving your healthy living if you want to succeed.

- Don't get overconfident about your health.
  - —Athletes are rarely satisfied about their performance: you should adopt this attitude as well. Keep your confidence in check and remember the key to a longer, healthy life is prudence and persistence.

- Give yourself a pessimistic health forecast.
  - —This is not suggesting you should believe you are going to die soon or with poor general health. Tell yourself you are going to need to stay on top of your health if you want to increase the chances of a positive life forecast.

—If you believe you will live a long, healthy life no matter what, what challenges will you have to overcome? What is going to motivate you to adopt a healthy lifestyle now?

- Accept that you are the cause of your health issues and that you are the solution.

- Embrace your low confidence! It will drive the important health changes you need to make.

8

Easier Said Than Done?

There are lots of ways of being miserable, but there's only one way of being comfortable, and that is to stop running round after happiness. If you make up your mind not to be happy there's no reason why you shouldn't have a fairly good time.

—Edith Wharton (1862–1937)

All You Need Is a Bit of Willpower (and Low Confidence)

Almost everything in life is easier said than done, but the key suggestions made in this book are easily translated into action. You don't have to make any radical transformations—all you need is to become a slightly more attuned version of yourself. This final chapter explains why and how you should be able to make this happen, and on a larger scale, what a less confident but more competent world would look like.

In 500 BCE, Socrates concluded that the key to happiness is discovering our true self. However, in the past five decades or so, the quest for happiness has caused a great deal of Western civilization, especially America, to distort their true selves in order to replace them with more confident versions. Although thinking that we are better than we actually are may make us feel good, a society that needs to comfort itself with ignorance for failing to accomplish its goals is a culture in decline, a spoiled society that has traded off competence for confidence and replaced reality with delusional success.

The typical self-help and coaching interventions designed to boost people's confidence are the product of this feel-good epidemic, and they are based on two false assumptions: first, that increasing our confidence will bring us success; second, that we all have the power to feel confident if we decide to. As shown throughout this book, there is no evidence that high confidence causes success, and even if it did, it is very hard to change our confidence levels and self-views arbitrarily and intentionally. This is why, upon reviewing decades of professional interventions designed to enhance people's self-esteem, Dr. Roy Baumeister concluded just that. He indicated that no evidence had been found to support the claim that, for example, through the use of therapeutic interventions or school programs, increasing self-esteem will produce benefits.[1]

Rather, hundreds of psychological studies show that deliberate attempts to suppress negative self-views backfire. For instance, trying to avoid unwanted thoughts or sensations, a process called "experiential avoidance," enhances the adverse effects of the very thoughts and sensations we try to avoid. In fact, experiential avoidance is a bigger threat to our mental health than the actual negative thoughts and feelings it attempts to suppress, as well as the events from which these thoughts and feelings arise. As stated by Dr. Todd Kashdan and his colleagues at George Mason University, we will all experience unwanted, uncomfortable moments including pain, suffering, and panic. However, these moments are part of our human nature and are not necessarily a problem. Moreover, experiential avoidance tends to get people into trouble, since they have to come into contact with sometimes rather painful emotional content. [2]

Thus, thoughts become problematic and disruptive only when you try to suppress them. Consider some of the well-documented manifestations of thought suppression:

- Juries' decisions on cases are usually affected by information they have been specifically asked to disregard, which is why lawyers will often make fake claims in court.[3]

- Audiences are still influenced by news stories they are told are false,[4] which is why fake rumors about political or public figures will damage their reputations even if later refuted.

- People's financial and gambling decisions are influenced by odds they deliberately try to ignore (even when they are offered money to do so).[5] For instance, people are more likely to buy a product for a hundred dollars if they see that it's discounted by 50 percent than buy the same product for seventy-five dollars when the discount is "only" 30 percent.

- Attempts to avoid food thoughts enhance subsequent worries about food, which is why aggressive dieting is often followed by binge eating and, in turn, obesity.[6]

- Attempts to avoid thinking about an upcoming surgery increase the probability of experiencing surgery-related stress later on.[7]

- Suppressing emotions connected to traumatic events causes more health problems than dealing with the unpleasant thoughts and emotions the event evokes.[8]

- The tendency to suppress negative emotions inhibits the experience of positive or pleasurable emotions.[9]

- Attempting to suppress negative thoughts is mentally draining, a bit like when heavy software consumes your PC's memory resources.[10]

- People who try to suppress racial stereotypes end up acting in a more prejudiced way than those who don't.[11]

Embracing Low Confidence

Suppression attempts backfire and stop you from taking the much-needed first steps to achieve self-improvement. The inability to fully engage with and accept unpleasant thoughts seriously harms your chances of becoming more competent, as well as distorting both your view of reality and of yourself. For example, if you are feeling worthless and try to suppress those feelings, you will never be able to do what it takes to improve. If, on the other hand, you come to terms with your negative self-views and accept the fact that you are not as good as you would like to be and, especially, that you are unhappy with yourself, you will be able to focus on what you need to do to improve. Dissatisfaction is the mother of change, and only change can drive improvement.

The choice between the two options is a no-brainer. Deliberate attempts to increase your confidence are bound to result in failure and demoralize you, whereas attempts to improve your performance can result in not just competence gains but also a genuine boost to your confidence.[12] In line, the answer to the question "What should I do about my low confidence?" could hardly be simpler:

Embrace it.

All that we've covered in this book so far points to the idea that you should not worry about your low confidence or try to eradicate it. Low confidence is what allows us to acknowledge our imperfections, our problems, and our worries. Acknowledging these things means that we can motivate ourselves to make changes and improve certain aspects of our lives and competencies within different domains.

This advice alone will prove to be a more effective confidence antidote than 99 percent of the suggestions you will find in popular self-help books. Indeed, your insecurities can only make you better, unless you choose to ignore them—only those who are in denial about their weaknesses miss the opportunity to capitalize on their lower self-confidence. For them, there is little hope; for you—given that you are reading this book and that you have gotten this far—there is not just hope but a realistic probability that you will turn your lower confidence into higher competence. The time has come to regard your lower confidence as an honest friend who may be too honest for your liking but has only your best interests at heart: He wants to help you improve. Furthermore, it is time to understand that the only genuine antidote to low confidence is to actually improve—that is, to gain competence. If you want a proper cure for your insecurities there is only one effective recipe: success.

Success Is the Best Medicine for Your Insecurities

Alfred Adler, one of Freud's early disciples (and later rivals), saw ambition as the quintessential attempt to overcome our insecurities. The more competitive people are, he argued, the more insecure they are underneath, such that displays of superiority can be interpreted as compensatory mechanisms for an underlying inferiority complex. Thus, low confidence is a problem only if you don't care enough about it to attempt to gain competence.

One thing I can see that high achievers have in common is that they self-medicate their insecurities with success. Indeed, although we are repeatedly told that exceptional achievers owe their success to their high confidence or self-belief, it is more feasible to attribute it to their insecurity—why else would anybody work so hard, and continue to work hard even after accomplishing much more than most people? In that sense, one could argue that the only difference between successful and unsuccessful people is that the former care much more about their insecurities, so they are driven to work hard to overcome them. And the key point is that they *work*, not on their insecurities, but on achieving big things; success is the best medicine.

People sometimes think I'm confident, but only because I fake it. Deep inside, I am certain of nothing and believe only in working hard for what I want. I hardly ever feel overconfident, but focus on my insecurities to push me to work harder instead of putting the energy toward improving my confidence. Although I have done reasonably well in my career, I would be devastated if I felt I had already reached my biggest accomplishments; the thought of complacency scares me. Thus, insecurities lead to ambition, which eclipses low confidence by focusing your attention on your goals rather than yourself, leading to higher levels of achievement, which in turn can give you realistic confidence. Conversely, the security and confidence that may result from having things too easy or being overly pleased with yourself are likely to hinder ambition and threaten potential improvements.

Another example is the Dutch soccer player Robin van Persie, who plays in England's Premier League for Manchester United. He has just embarked on his first season at the club and has had a rather incredible start. He is scoring amazing goals week in, week out, and has effectively won the title for his new club. However, when interviewed about his perfect start with his new team, he talks about the *missed* goals he was responsible for and the *faults* he perceived in his game. He insisted that, while he is enjoying himself, he is very aware of the things he has to work on in order to better his performance. This is why he is doing so well. He works incredibly hard, setting himself new targets and standards all the time, and he is happier now than he has ever been in his career. Becoming so competent in his role on the team and seeing the rewards for his hard work has led him to both success and happiness. And he's still in his twenties. . . .

When we tell people that they can achieve anything they want so long as they have high confidence, their motivation to work hard decreases. When we tell people that everybody is equally capable of achieving anything, we create in them high expectations and a false sense of entitlement, which reduces their willpower. In every domain of competence (e.g., education, careers, sports, relationships, and health), some people are naturally better endowed than others, in that they are pretty much born with an advantage over their peers. For example, being born to a wealthier family will give you access to better health and education; being naturally more physically attractive will make you a more desirable romantic partner; and a better genetic makeup will make you healthier and increase the probability of living longer. All these inborn characteristics are comparable to height, in that you cannot do much to alter them. If you think about confidence as height, and performance as jumping high, it should help you understand and remember one of the key lessons of this book: Even if you cannot alter your height, you can always learn to jump higher—and being born short should make you work extra hard to achieve your goals. And here's the beauty of it: Once you do, you will feel better about your height, too.

To stay with a sports metaphor: If you want to run like Usain Bolt—the fastest man on earth—you better start training now, train all the time, and stop doing anything else. It will also help if you avoid thinking that you have the same natural talent for running as Bolt does (even in the unlikely event that you do), because if you believe you do, you will be unaware of your limitations and likely train less. Most of us are average at what we do; being aware of this is especially useful if you want to be better than average. When you struggle, you need to be realistic about it in order to improve, and being fully aware of your problems is the biggest incentive to work hard to bring about positive change.

The contestants on *The Biggest Loser* are usually people who have been severely overweight since childhood. What is most interesting, from a psychological perspective, is that these people start with extremely low levels of self-esteem (as one would expect given their situation), yet season after season, they are willing to expose themselves intimately to millions of TV viewers, in an attempt to achieve something that is extremely difficult and totally outside their confidence zone. This is a wonderful example of how willpower, especially the desire to improve, trumps the inhibitory effects of low confidence. If you really want something, you will work hard to attain it. If what you want is to recover your confidence, then you should focus on improving your performance. Work hard on your accomplishments and your confidence will take care of itself.

A More Competent You

Most people like the idea of being exceptional, but not enough to do what it takes to get there. This is true for most domains of competence. For instance, everybody says that they want to be slim, healthy, attractive, and rich, but few people are willing to do what it takes to attain those things, which suggests that they don't *really* want those things as much as they say or think. Paul Arden, former creative director of Saatchi & Saatchi, sums this up nicely by explaining that typically when we say we "want" something, we actually just mean that we want to *have* it, but with no implicit assumption that we're willing to do any work to get there. In reality, wanting something should equate with being prepared to take the necessary steps to achieve it.[13] If you are serious about your goals, then you will do whatever it takes to attain them; your confidence is secondary. What matters is the desire you have to attempt to achieve them.

The fact that you have read this book demonstrates that you have already solved half of the problem, which is having the necessary willpower to improve. Indeed, without the will to improve there is no chance of accomplishing anything, and with enough willpower it is possible to overcome most challenges. So, you've bought this book, reached the last chapter, and are now equipped with tools to succeed, in addition to your determination. The advantage is yours—you are in pole position.

As you continue on this journey, be sure to use your low confidence as a potent weapon: It enables you to make a realistic assessment of your competence, keeping any delusions and self-enhancement in check; it helps you prepare for negative events, preventing failure; and it ensures that you come across as humble to others, which will make you more likable. Remember that most people lack this weapon. You can never be too aware of your weaknesses; as we know now, being aware of them is a major strength, while being aware only of your strengths—or erroneously thinking that you are better than average—will sooner or later turn into a weakness.

Regardless of the underlying reasons for your low confidence, it is clear that you want to improve—or at least you want to stop feeling that you lack competence. That's why low confidence is such a powerful weapon: Even in the unlikely event that it does not alter your perceived incompetence, it will still drive positive change. It is noteworthy, in this respect, that both low and high confidence disrupt the Confidence-Competence Cycle (as introduced in the first chapter), but only low confidence does so for your benefit. When your confidence is high, you will tend to decrease effort to gain competence (unless you do nothing at all, implying stagnation and recession, which are not much better options anyway). When it is low, you will be driven to increase your efforts to accomplish competence. In simple terms, the less confident you feel, the more you will be itching to improve, unless you don't care about your confidence. If you do care, and your low confidence is bugging you, then you really have no excuse!

As we've seen, low confidence is the essential fuel for gaining competence because it increases preparation, the key ingredient for any competence gains. If your low confidence is health related, then preparation means becoming a healthier person; if your low confidence relates to romantic relationships, then preparation implies becoming a more eligible partner; if you lack confidence in your ability to deal with people, then preparation means refining your people skills; and if your low confidence applies to your career, then preparation refers to enhancing your employability. There it is, in a nutshell.

In brief, so long as you have the necessary motivation to improve, not only before but also after you gain competence, you will be able to earn and deserve your confidence without distorting your beliefs or trying to go against your nature. Even if you don't change your confidence levels, society will benefit: Your lack of confidence is a much-needed antidote to the common incompetent confidence that rules our world. So long as you remain unconfident, there will be undeluded life on our planet. And in any event, try not to envy people who are confident—instead, make every effort to identify genuine competence manifestations in others, regardless of their confidence.

A More Competent, Less Confident World

Many problems in the modern world are the result of distorted confidence levels, more specifically overconfidence or incompetent confidence. The effects of this confidence surplus are indeed everywhere and too many to mention here, but let me give you a few real world examples, which would become only theoretical if competence gains eliminated the current gaps between confidence and competence.

Most political elections are essentially battles of confidence—the candidate who conveys a greater amount of self-belief ends up gaining the confidence of voters (this is especially true in the United States). The result is a vicious circle: Because it is disguised as competence, higher confidence is an important weapon to accumulate power, and the accumulation of power further increases confidence, giving people a false sense of security and increasing the propensity to take risks and lose touch with reality.[14] If more politicians were elected on competence rather than confidence, and, indeed, if confidence mattered less than competence in a candidate's political career, there would be fewer disappointments with the failures of politicians.

In his fascinating book, *Overconfidence and War*, Dominic Johnson argues that most wars can be understood primarily as the result of positive illusions—or delusions—of political leaders.[15] Indeed, countries would never go to war unless they thought that they could win, which is obviously impossible for both sides. A big difference between the Vietnam War and the Cuban missile crisis was overconfidence (which led to war) in the case of the former. As Johnson argues, a country and its leaders are as biased as its citizens . . . or even more: Politicians tend to be more confident and narcissistic than the average voter, particularly in the era of media politics. There is a famous saying that every country has the government it deserves—it is easy to see how voters who value confidence over competence will end up with leaders who are much more confident than competent, and vice versa.

Contrast Angela Merkel, the German chancellor, with Silvio Berlusconi, the former Italian prime minister. Merkel is an uncharismatic, low-key, dorky-looking leader; she has a PhD in physics and appears to be more suited for academia than politics. Berlusconi is a charismatic, narcissistic media entrepreneur and one of the richest men in Europe. Both were elected democratically and achieved stellar political heights. Merkel is the face of high competence coupled with low confidence (she is cautious, risk averse, unglamorous, and discreet); Berlusconi is the face of high confidence coupled with low competence, except when it comes to corruption. Now compare the state of the German and Italian economies. Additionally, consider the case of Argentina (my country of origin). Argentina was once one of the richest countries in the world, but today it is in steep decline.[16] Yet its decline is the natural consequence of combining incompetent confidence with an unrealistic sense of entitlement. Too confident in the power of its fertile land, the country became lax, taking ages to modernize. Rosendo Fraga, a political analyst, argues that as a country, Argentina needs to look to Chile or Uruguay as role models to make changes (become a simpler, more austere country), instead of acting like the country of 1913.

The 2008 economic meltdown has managed to draw many people's attention to the toxic effect of high confidence. Unsurprisingly, there has been a recent increase in research into the detrimental results of unrealistic optimism and delusional confidence. For example, a group of European researchers led by Nihat Aktas at Emlyon Business School, in France, found that narcissistic CEOs tend to make more aggressive takeovers, and at higher prices, disrupting the market and damaging their company. This finding is consistent with a well-known management paradox: The factors that enable executives to climb the corporate ladder are inversely related to the factors that enable managers to become good leaders. To make it to the top, it is often essential to be greedy and arrogant, but to be a good leader—even in the corporate world—you need to be a team player and modest.[17]

The detrimental effects of high confidence are most noticeable when we analyze the historical movements of upward and downward social mobility—that is, generational increases or decreases in socioeconomic status. When people are driven and ambitious, they tend to attain higher levels of prosperity than their parents. Throughout history, migrants have tended to escape abuses in human rights, repressive regimes, poverty, and unpromising economic forecasts in their home countries, such that migration is always motivated by insecurity or a lack of confidence in the future. Even among fairly educated and affluent migrants, the lack of confidence in their own country is such that they are happy to downgrade their socioeconomic status in their adoptive country. But most migrants tend to capitalize on their ambition and soon improve their living conditions relative to what they were at home. In some cases, this will allow them to send their children—who are usually born in the adoptive country—to better schools and universities, allowing them to increase their socioeconomic status even further. Yet the next generation of children will often have it too easy, which may make them spoiled and less hungry for success. Growing up in stable, happy, and secure households may end up killing ambition, which leads to downward social mobility. The most extreme examples of this are found in aristocratic families, in which the amount of inherited wealth tends to decline with every generation. If you think these trends apply just to aristocratic and monarchic regimes, think again. Recent data suggests that more than one-third of U.S. citizens born to middle class families in the 1960s have downgraded their socioeconomic status[18]—and this was way before the subprime lending catastrophe of 2008.

Final Thoughts

The search for meaning is a defining feature of humankind, as the great psychoanalyst Carl Jung noted. Although life can be painful, meaning can help us alleviate the pain. But when meaning depends on constructing an artificial account of ourselves in order to make ourselves feel better about our failures, then bad things are bound to occur. As we now know, it is low confidence that acts as the source of success.

What would a less confident world look like?

People would start each day being better prepared; there would be fewer arguments and fewer mistakes. Politicians and military leaders would hesitate before sending us to war, CEOs would be less corrupt, and drivers would be more careful. Indeed, many of the major global disasters of the past few decades, which have been attributed to confidence excess, might never have happened. In line, the world would be a more competent place if we could lower people's confidence.

According to Alfred Adler, "To be human is to feel inferior." Perhaps, but competence gains relieve our natural feelings of inferiority, at least temporarily. Indeed, inferiority *motivates* us to try to achieve things. The more weaknesses you perceive in yourself, the more you will be motivated to improve, and the harder you will work. Low confidence is the result of failure but the source of success.

Acknowledgments

I am grateful to my agent, Giles Anderson, and Caroline Sutton and Christina Rodriguez at Penguin, for helping me interpret my thoughts and making this book possible; my outstanding research assistants, Lauren Carter, Sian Conner, and Natasha Kousseff, for their 24-7 support; and my patient wife, Mylène Spence, for tolerating my long working hours (and me) during this project.

Notes

Dear Reader

1. Collectivistic societies, like Japan, do not worship confidence like we do in the West, and even in the Western world the obsession with high confidence is fairly recent. For instance, in the Jewish-Christian tradition humility is considered much more virtuous than hubris; in the Middle Ages, pride was regarded as a satanic sin and avoided at all costs.

Chapter 1: Confidence Ain't Competence

1. You can find thousands of others, for instance if you Google "confidence" and "success."
2. R. Lubit, "The Long-Term Organizational Impact of Destructively Narcissistic Managers," *Academy of Management Executive* 16, no. 1 (2002): 127–38.
3. J. M. Twenge and W. K. Campbell, *The Narcissism Epidemic: Living in the Age of Entitlement* (New York: Free Press, 2009).
4. N. Galambos, E. Barker, and H. Krahn, "Depression, Self-esteem, and Anger in Emerging Adulthood: Seven-Year Trajectories," *Developmental Psychology* 42, no. 2 (2006): 350–65.

5. F. S. Stinson, D. A. Dawson, R. B. Goldstein, S. P. Chou, B. Huang, S. M. Smith, W. J. Ruan, et al., "Prevalence, Correlates, Disability, and Comorbidity of DSM-IV Narcissistic Personality Disorder: Results from the Wave 2 National Epidemiologic Survey on Alcohol and Related Conditions," *Journal of Clinical Psychiatry* 69, no. 7, (2008): 1033–45.

6. Jeffrey Kluger, "How America's Children Packed on the Pounds," *Time*, June 12, 2008. Read more: http://www.livestrong.com/article/384722-how-much-have-obesity-rates-risen-since-1950/#ixzz20Ef9NhvT.

7. See, for instance, P. Kirschner and A. Karpinski, "Facebook and Academic Performance," *Computers in Human Behavior* 26, no. 6 (2010): 1237–45.

8. Facebook does allow users to "like" their own activity. As a recent post jokingly noted, "Why does Facebook even give me the option to 'like' my own status? Of course I like my own status, I'm f**** hilarious! And sexy." If only this were just a joke . . .

9. T. Ryan and S. Xenos, "Who Uses Facebook? An Investigation into the Relationship Between the Big Five, Shyness, Narcissism, Loneliness, and Facebook Usage," *Computers in Human Behavior* 27, no. 5 (2011): 1658–64.

10. W. Compton, K. Conway, F. Stinson, and B. Grant, "Changes in the Prevalence of Major Depression and Comorbid Substance Use Disorders in the United States Between 1991–1992 and 2001–2002," *American Journal of Psychiatry* 163, no. 12 (2006): 2141–47.

11. G. Parker, G. Gladstone, and K. T. Chee, "Depression in the Planet's Largest Ethnic Group: the Chinese," *American Journal of Psychiatry* 158, no. 6 (2001): 857–64.

12. "Health Topics: Depression," World Health Organization, http://www.who.int/topics/depression/en/.

13. At the time of writing this chapter, Coke had 41,344,619 "likes" on Facebook.

14. What the marketing geniuses at Coca-Cola understood so well is that in a narcissistic society people love to feel good about themselves. This is what made Coca-Cola the most recognizable brand on the

planet—the logo is apparently recognized by 94 percent of the world's population. You may think this is because of how good Coke tastes, but do you really believe Pepsi tastes that much worse? Coke's success is based not on the alleged secret recipe for its drink, but on smart branding and its ability to appeal to an increasingly narcissistic culture.

15. N. Herr, "Television & Health," Internet Resources to Accompany the Sourcebook for Teaching Science, http://www.csun.edu/science/ health/docs/tv&health.html.

16. Marketdata Enterprises, "Self-improvement Market Growth Slows, as Recession Takes Toll and Consumers Await the Next Big Thing," press release, October 14, 2008.

17. K. Schulz, "The Self in Self-help," *New York*, January 6, 2013, http:// nymag.com/health/self-help/2013/schulz-self-searching/.

18. S. Salerno, *SHAM: How the Self-help Movement Made America Helpless* (New York: Crown Publishers, 2005).

19. R. F. Baumeister, J. D. Campbell, J. I. Krueger, and K. D. Vohs, "Does High Self-esteem Cause Better Performance, Interpersonal Success, Happiness, or Healthier Lifestyles?" *Psychological Science in the Public Interest* 4, no. 1 (2003): 1–44.

20. When a correlation is 0, the probability of one event happening when the other one happens (e.g., being competent when you appear confident) is 50 percent—the chance rate. But to translate other correlations into yes-or-no probabilities, you just divide the correlation coefficient by 2 and add the resulting number to the chance rate (the 50 percent baseline). Since the correlation between confidence and competence is .30, the probability of one event happening when the other one happens is 65 percent (30/2 = 15 + 50 = 65).

21. Baumeister et al., "Does High Self-esteem Cause Better Performance," 7.

22. E. Diener, B. Wolsic, and F. Fujita, "Physical Attractiveness and Subjective Well-being," *Journal of Personality and Social Psychology* 69, no. 1 (1995): 120–29.

23. Baumeister et al., "Does High Self-esteem Cause Better Performance," 8.

24. I. Schmidt, I. Berg, and B. Deelman, "Prospective Memory Training in Older Adults," *Educational Gerontology* 27, no. 6 (2001): 455–78.
25. V. Hoorens and P. Harris, "Distortions in Reports of Health Behaviors: The Time Span Effect and Illusory Superiority," *Psychology and Health* 13, no. 3 (1998): 451–66.
26. L. Larwood and W. Whittaker, "Managerial Myopia: Self-serving Biases in Organizational Planning," *Journal of Applied Psychology* 62, no. 2 (1977): 194–98.
27. R. B. Felson, "Ambiguity and Bias in the Self-concept," *Social Psychology Quarterly* 44, no. 1 (1981): 64–69.
28. Y. Endo, S. Heine, and D. Lehman, "Culture and Positive Illusions in Close Relationships: How My Relationships Are Better Than Yours," *Personality and Social Psychology Bulletin* 26, no. 12 (2000): 1571–86.
29. O. Svenson, "Are We All Less Risky and More Skillful Than Our Fellow Drivers?" *Acta Psychologica* 47, no. 2 (1981): 143–48.
30. College Board, "Student Descriptive Questionnaire" (Princeton, NJ: Educational Testing Service, 1976–1977).
31. K. P. Cross, "Not Can, But *Will* College Teaching Be Improved?" *New Directions for Higher Education* 17 (1977): 1–15.
32. Of course, it is not always impossible for most people to be better than average. For example, most people have more legs than the average person—the small number of people who have just one leg or none bring the average number of legs down to less than two. The same occurs when data are positively skewed, which implies that most people will be below average. A common example for this is income: Most people tend to earn less than the average salary, because the average salary is inflated by a small number of mega-rich people. More often than not, however, variables are normally distributed, which makes the statistical average roughly equal to the midpoint of the scale, as well as the most frequent value.

33. J. Friedrich,"On Seeing Oneself as Less Self-serving Than Others: The Ultimate Self-serving Bias?" *Teaching of Psychology* 23, no. 2 (1996): 107–9.

34. E. Pronin, D. Y. Lin, and L. Ross, "The Bias Blind Spot: Perceptions of Bias in Self Versus Others," *Personality and Social Psychology Bulletin* 28, no. 3 (2002): 369–81.

35. Ibid., 378.

36. T. Sharot, "The Optimism Bias," *Current Biology* 21, no. 23 (2011): R941–45.

37. University of California, San Diego, "California's Leadership in Tobacco Control Resulted in Lower Lung Cancer Rate, Study Finds," ScienceDaily, September 29, 2010, http://www.sciencedaily.com/releases/2010/09/100929142131.htm.

38. D. Thompson, *The Fix* (London, UK: Harper Collins, 2012).

39. C. Colvin, J. Block, and D. C. Funder, "Overly Positive Self-Evaluations and Personality: Negative Implications for Mental Health," *Journal of Personality and Social Psychology* 68, no. 6 (1995): 1152–62.

40. Ibid., 1156.

41. Ibid., 1159.

42. R. Trivers, *The Folly of Fools: The Logic of Deceit and Self-deception in Human Life* (New York: Basic Books, 2011).

43. K. H. Lambird and T. Mann, "When Do Ego Threats Lead to Self-regulation Failure? Negative Consequences of Defensive High Self-esteem," *Personality and Social Psychology Bulletin* 32, no. 9 (2006): 1177–87.

44. D. L. Paulhus, P. D. Harms, M. N. Bruce, and D. C. Lysy, "The Over-Claiming Technique: Measuring Self-enhancement Independent of Ability," *Journal of Personality and Social Psychology* 84, no. 4 (2003): 890–904.

45. Unsurprisingly, depression is not uncommon in exceptional achievers—for example, Woody Allen, Charles Dickens, Fyodor Dostoyevsky, Harrison Ford, and Michelangelo all reportedly

suffered from it. Another salient case was Friedrich Nietzsche, who famously stated, "Whatever does not kill me makes me stronger"— not a bad take on depression!

46. P. W. Andrews and J. A. Thomson Jr., "The Bright Side of Being Blue: Depression as an Adaptation for Analyzing Complex Problems," *Psychological Review* 116, no. 3 (2009): 620–54.

Chapter 2: Taking Advantage of Low Confidence

1. D. H. Barlow, *Anxiety and Its Disorders: The Nature and Treatment of Anxiety and Panic*, 2nd ed. (New York: Guilford Press, 2002).
2. D. H. Zald and J. V. Pardo, "Emotion, Olfaction, and the Human Amygdala: Amygdala Activation During Aversive Olfactory Stimulation," *Proceedings of the National Academy of Sciences of the United States of America* 94, no. 8 (1997): 4119–24.
3. W. E. Lee, M. E. Wadsworth, and M. Hotopf, "The Protective Role of Trait Anxiety: A Longitudinal Cohort Study," *Psychological Medicine* 36, no. 3 (2006): 345–51.
4. M. O. Johnson, "HIV Vaccine Volunteers: Personality, Motivation and Risk," ProQuest Information & Learning, AAM9839840 (1999).
5. P. Simpson-Housley, A. F. De Man, and R. Yachnin, "Trait-Anxiety and Appraisal of Flood Hazard: A Brief Comment," *Psychological Reports* 58, no. 2 (1986): 509–10.
6. See chapter 7 for details.
7. I. M. Marks and R. M. Nesse, "Fear and Fitness: An Evolutionary Analysis of Anxiety Disorders," *Ethology and Sociobiology* 15 (1994): 247–61.
8. "Statistics," National Institute of Mental Health, http://www.nimh.nih.gov/statistics/.
9. C. Blanco, M. Okuda, C. Wright, D. S. Hasin, B. F. Grant, S. M. Liu, and M. Olfson, "Mental Health of College Students and Their Non-College Attending Peers: Results from the National Epidemiologic Study on Alcohol and Related Conditions," *Archives of General Psychiatry* 65, no. 12 (2008): 1429–37.

10. K. Belzer and F. Schneier, "Comorbidity of Anxiety and Depressive Disorders: Issues in Conceptualization, Assessment, and Treatment," *Journal of Psychiatric Practice* 10, no. 5 (2004): 296–306.

11. E. Gut, *Productive and Unproductive Depression: Success or Failure of a Vital Process* (New York: Basic Books, 1989).

12. D. Nettle, "Evolutionary Origins of Depression: A Review and Reformulation," *Journal of Affective Disorders* 81, no. 2 (2004): 91–102.

13. L. B. Alloy and L. Y. Abramson, "Judgment of Contingency in Depressed and Nondepressed Students: Sadder but Wiser?" *Journal of Experimental Psychology: General* 108, no. 4 (1979): 441–85; K. Dobson and R. Franche, "A Conceptual and Empirical Review of the Depressive Realism Hypothesis," *Canadian Journal of Behavioural Science* 21, no. 4 (1989): 419–33.

14. R. L. Leahy, "Pessimism and the Evolution of Negativity," *Journal of Cognitive Psychotherapy* 16, no. 3 (2002): 295–316.

15. Marks and Nesse, "Fear and Fitness," 254.

16. S. Tzu, *The Art of War* (New York: SoHo, 2010), 20.

17. T. Gilovich, *How We Know What Isn't So: The Fallibility of Human Reason in Everyday Life* (New York: Free Press, 1991).

18. "Male Traders Are from Mars," *Economist*, May 18, 2009, http://www.economist.com/blogs/freeexchange/2009/05/male_traders_are_from_mars.

19. J. M. Coates and J. Herbert, "Endogenous Steroids and Financial Risk Taking on a London Trading Floor," *Proceedings of the National Academy of Sciences of the United States of America* 105, no. 16 (2008): 6167–72.

20. V. H. Galbraith, *The Making of Domesday Book* (London: Clarendon Press, 1961), 30.

21. J. Lammers, J. Stoker, J. Jordan, M. Pollman, and D. Stapel, "Power Increases Infidelity Among Men and Women," *Psychological Science* 22, no. 9 (2011): 1191–97.

22. J. Polivy and C. Herman, "If at First You Don't Succeed: False Hopes of Self-Change," *American Psychologist* 57, no. 9 (2002): 677–89.

23. D. Cervone and P. K. Peake, "Anchoring, Efficacy, and Action: The
    Influence of Judgmental Heuristics on Self-Efficacy Judgments and
    Behavior," *Journal of Personality and Social Psychology* 50, no. 3
    (1986): 492–501.
24. W. T. Powers,"Commentary on Bandura's 'Human Agency,'"
    American Psychologist 46, no. 2 (1991): 151–53.
25. J. B. Vancouver, C. M. Thompson, E. C. Tischner, and D. J. Putka,
    "Two Studies Examining the Negative Effect of Self-Efficacy on
    Performance," *Journal of Applied Psychology* 87, no. 3 (2002): 506–16.
26. D. N. Stone, "Overconfidence in Initial Self-Efficacy Judgments:
    Effects on Decision Processes and Performance," *Organizational
    Behavior and Human Decision Processes* 59, no. 3 (1994): 452–74.
27. W. T. Powers, *Behavior: The Control of Perception* (Chicago: Aldine,
    1973).
28. J. T. Austin and J. B. Vancouver, "Goal Constructs in Psychology:
    Structure, Process, and Content," *Psychological Bulletin* 120, no. 3
    (1996): 338–75.
29. D. Carnegie, *How to Win Friends and Influence People* (London:
    Cedar, 1953), 103.
30. "Johnny Depp Quote," Said What?, http://www.saidwhat.co.uk/
    quotes/celebrity/johnny_depp/my_self-image_it_still_isnt_that_751.
31. Cara Lee, "Robbie: I Wasn't on Drugs," *Sun*, October 20, 2009,
    http://www.thesun.co.uk/sol/homepage/showbiz/tv/x_factor/
    2690850/Robbie-Williams-I-wasnt-on-drugs.html?.
32. Cristina Everett, "Demi Moore Reveals Her Biggest Fear Is She's
    'Not Worthy of Being Loved': Actress Calls Herself a 'Warrior' After
    Ashton Kutcher Split," *Daily News*, January 4, 2012, http://articles
    .nydailynews.com/2012-01-04/news/30590839_1_scares-demi-
    moore-moore-talks.
33. There is a pathological manifestation of the "fake it till you make it"
    principle, namely the "impostor syndrome." Individuals affected by
    this syndrome systematically disbelieve that their success is
    deserved, thinking instead that other people have been fooled into

believing that they are competent, when they don't see themselves as competent enough. The syndrome is an example of persuading others of our competence without persuading ourselves. A less extreme version of this syndrome would not be a bad approach to dealing with confidence.

34. C. F. Bond Jr. and B. M. DePaulo, "Accuracy of Deception Judgements," *Personality and Social Psychology Review* 10, no. 3 (2006): 214–34.

35. Ibid., 214.

Chapter 3: Reputation Is King

1. Some of our emotions—the ones that are hardest to control and most intense—still reflect the evolutionary link between confidence and competence. When we are embarrassed, we blush, and the more we try to avoid it, the more we end up blushing. Equally, when we are stressed or excited, we spontaneously communicate fear or joy to others, and so on.

2. E. Pronin and M. B. Kugler, "People Believe They Have More Free Will Than Others," *Proceedings of the National Academy of Sciences of the United States of America* 107, no. 52 (2010): 22469–74.

3. N. M. Kierein and M. A. Gold, "Pygmalion in Work Organizations: A Meta-analysis," *Journal of Organizational Behavior* 21, no. 8 (2000): 913–28.

4. T. Chamorro-Premuzic, *Personality and Individual Differences*, 2nd ed. (Oxford, UK: Wiley-Blackwell, 2011).

5. There is arguably no stronger demonstration of this rule than the sad case of gender-based abortion. In countries such as India, South Korea, and China, there are now a disproportionate number of males relative to females, and this unnatural selection is caused by parents' belief that sons will be more competent than daughters. See M. Hvistendahl, *Unnatural Selection: The Consequences of Choosing Boys over Girls* (New York: Public Affairs, 2011).

6. A. M. Koenig, A. H. Eagly, A. A. Mitchell, and T. Ristikari, "Are Leader Stereotypes Masculine? A Meta-analysis of Three Research Paradigms," *Psychological Bulletin* 137, no. 4 (2011): 616–42.

7. S. Wellington, M. B. Kropf, and P. R. Gerkovich, "What's Holding Women Back?" *Harvard Business Review* 81, no. 6 (2003): 18–19.

8. W. Wosinska, A. J. Dabul, R. Whetstone-Dion, and R. B. Cialdini, "Self-Presentational Responses to Success in the Organization: The Costs and Benefits of Modesty," *Basic and Applied Social Psychology* 18, no. 2 (1996): 229–42.

9. By the way, this sex difference can be attributed to the fact that extreme modesty is both more common and more genuine in women than in men.

10. Wosinska et al., "Self-Presentational Responses to Success," 239.

11. J. Collins, "Level 5 Leadership: The Triumph of Humility and Fierce Resolve," *Harvard Business Review* 79, no. 1 (2001): 67–76.

12. For a detailed discussion of the importance of inferring intention, see G. D. Reeder, "Mindreading: Judgments About Intentionality and Motives in Dispositional Inference," *Psychological Inquiry* 20, no. 1 (2009): 1–18.

13. B. S. Connelly and D. S. Ones, "An Other Perspective on Personality: Meta-analytic Integration of Observers' Accuracy and Predictive Validity," *Psychological Bulletin* 136, no. 6 (2010): 1092–122.

14. You should try this: Ask your friends how they see you and you will see that they are mostly in agreement, even when you are not.

15. C. H. Cooley, *Human Nature and the Social Order* (New York: Schreiber, 1902).

16. G. H. Mead and D. L. Miller, *The Individual and the Social Self: Unpublished Work of George Herbert Mead* (Chicago: University of Chicago Press, 1982), 5.

17. M. Leary, "Motivational and Emotional Aspects of the Self," *Annual Review of Psychology* 58 (2007): 317–44.

18. J. S. Beer and D. Keltner, "What Is Unique About Self-Conscious Emotions?" *Psychological Inquiry* 15, no. 2 (2004): 126–70.

19. A. H. Baumgardner, C. M. Kaufman, and P. E. Levy, "Regulating Affect Interpersonally: When Low Esteem Leads to Greater Enhancement," *Journal of Personality and Social Psychology* 56, no. 6 (1989): 907–21.

20. R. F. Baumeister, "A Self-Presentational View of Social Phenomena," *Psychological Bulletin* 91, no. 1 (1982): 3–26.

21. L. H. Somerville, W. M. Kelley, and T. F. Heatherton, "Self-esteem Modulates Medial Prefrontal Cortical Responses to Evaluative Social Feedback," *Cerebral Cortex* 20, no. 12 (2010): 3005–13.

22. T. Sharot, C. W. Korn, and R. J. Dolan, "How Unrealistic Optimism Is Maintained in the Face of Reality," *Nature Neuroscience* 14, no. 11 (2011): 1475–79.

23. On May 24, 2006, the show received 63 million votes, almost 10 million more than the most widely voted president in U.S. history (Ronald Reagan in the 1984 election).

Chapter 4: A Successful Career

1. C. U. Greven, N. Harlaar, Y. Kovas, T. Chamorro-Premuzic, and R. Plomin, "More Than Just IQ: School Achievement Is Predicted by Self-Perceived Abilities—But for Genetic Rather Than Environmental Reasons," *Psychological Science* 20, no. 6 (2009): 753–62; T. Chamorro-Premuzic, N. Harlaar, C. U. Greven, and R. Plomin, "More Than Just IQ: A Longitudinal Examination of Self-Perceived Abilities as Predictors of Academic Performance in a Large Sample of UK Twins," *Intelligence* 38, no. 4 (2010): 385–92.

2. T. Chamorro-Premuzic and A. Furnham, *Personality and Intellectual Competence* (Mahwah, NJ: Lawrence Erlbaum Associates, 2005).

3. Rather than disrespecting one of today's corporate icons, I am just stating a fact—and Mark Zuckerberg seems perfectly aware of his limitations as a corporate leader, given that he has hired the impressive Sheryl Sandberg (former VP at Google) to run Facebook's operations. That said, Facebook valuation appears to be more a matter of confidence than competence.

4. T. Chamorro-Premuzic and A. Furnham, *The Psychology of Personnel Selection* (New York: Cambridge University Press, 2010).

5. R. Hogan and R. Kaiser, "How to Assess Integrity," *Consulting Psychology Journal* (forthcoming).

6. Chamorro-Premuzic, *Personality and Individual Differences*.

7. "Strategic Consulting," Gallup, http://www.gallup.com/consulting/52/employee-engagement.aspx/.

8. J. Hillard and E. Pollard, *Employability: Developing a Framework for Policy Analysis* (Nottingham, UK: Department of Education and Employment, 1998).

9. "Civilian Labor Force Participation Rate," Bureau of Labor Statistics, http://data.bls.gov/timeseries/LNS11300000years_option=specific_years&include_graphs=true&to_month=1&from_month=2.

10. "The Joyless or the Jobless," *Economist*, November 25, 2010.

11. Y. Baruch and N. Bozionelos, "Career Issues," in *Handbook of Industrial and Organizational Psychology*, Vol. 2, ed. S. Zedeck (Washington, DC: American Psychological Association, 2011), 67–133.

12. Chamorro-Premuzic and Furnham, *Personality and Intellectual Competence*.

13. T. Chamorro-Premuzic and A. Furnham, "Intellectual Competence and the Intelligent Personality: A Third Way in Differential Psychology," *Review of General Psychology* 10, no. 3 (2006): 251–67.

14. C. Mueller and C. Dweck, "Praise for Intelligence Can Undermine Children's Motivation and Performance," *Journal of Personality and Social Psychology* 75, no. 1 (1998): 33–42.

15. M. Gladwell, *Outliers: The Story of Success* (New York: Little, Brown, 2008).

16. A. K. Ericsson, N. Charness, P. Feltovich, and R. R. Hoffman, *The Cambridge Handbook of Expertise and Expert Performance* (Cambridge, UK: Cambridge University Press, 2006).

17. B. Tulgan, *Winning the Talent Wars: How to Build a Lean, Flexible, High-Performance Workplace* (New York: W. W. Norton, 2001).

18. P. Brown and A. Hesketh, *The Mismanagement of Talent: Employability and Jobs in the Knowledge Economy* (Oxford, UK: Oxford University Press, 2004), 153.

19. R. Hogan, T. Chamorro-Premuzic, and R. Kaiser, "Employablity: Who Can Get and Keep a Job?" *Perspectives of Industrial-Organizational Psychology* (forthcoming).

20. Ibid.

21. Gallup, "Strategic Consulting."

22. "Store: Level 5 Leadership: The Triumph of Humility and Fierce Resolve (HBR Classic)," *Harvard Business Review,* http://hbr.org/product/level-5-leadership-the-triumph-of-humility-and-fie/an/R0507M-PDF-ENG.

23. R. Hogan, *Personality and the Fate of Organizations* (Mahwah, NJ: Lawrence Erlbaum Associates, 2007).

24. T. A. Judge, J. E. Bono, R. Ilies, and M. W. Gerhardt, "Personality and Leadership: A Qualitative and Quantitative Review," *Journal of Applied Psychology* 87, no. 4 (2002): 765–80.

25. Naturally, being nice does not always pay off. In fact, recent data suggests that men who come across as kind and considerate often end up earning less than their more argumentative and confrontational counterparts (see T. A. Judge, B. A. Livingstone, and C. Hurst, "Do Nice Guys—and Gals—Really Finish Last? The Joint Effects of Sex and Agreeableness on Income," *Journal of Personality and Social Psychology* 102, no. 2 [2012]: 390–407). However, being unrewarding to deal with is counterproductive to achieving success in any career.

26. B. Dattner, *The Blame Game: How the Hidden Rules of Credit and Blame Determine Our Success or Failure* (New York: Simon & Schuster, 2011), 52.

Chapter 5: Social Confidence and People Skills

1. P. A. Mabe and S. G. West, "Validity of Self-evaluation of Ability: A Review and Meta-analysis," *Journal of Applied Psychology* 67, no. 3 (1982): 280–96.

2. B. M. DePaulo, K. Charlton, H, Cooper, J. J. Lindsay, and L. Muhlenbruck, "The Accuracy-Confidence Correlation in the Detection of Deception," *Personality and Social Psychology Review* 1, no. 4 (1997): 346–57.

3. J. Brockner and A. J. Blethyn Hulton, "How to Reverse the Vicious Cycle of Low Self-esteem: The Importance of Attentional Focus," *Journal of Experimental Social Psychology* 14, no. 6 (1978): 564–78.

4. J. A. Bishop and H. M. Inderbitzen, "Peer Acceptance and Friendship: An Investigation of Their Relation to Self-esteem," *Journal of Early Adolescence* 15, no. 4 (1995): 476–89.

5. These findings were replicated by M. M. Dolcini and N. E. Adler in "Perceived Competencies, Peer Group Affiliation, and Risk Behavior Among Early Adolescents," *Health Psychology* 13, no. 6 (1994): 496–506.

6. G. R. Adams, B. A. Ryan, M. Ketsetzis, and L. Keating, "Rule Compliance and Peer Sociability: A Study of Family Process, School-Focused Parent-Child Interactions, and Children's Classroom Behavior," *Journal of Family Psychology* 14, no. 2 (2000): 237–50.

7. D. Buhrmester, W. Furman, M. T. Wittenberg, and H. T. Reis, "Five Domains of Interpersonal Competence in Peer Relationships," *Journal of Personality and Social Psychology* 55, no. 6 (1988): 991–1008.

8. Baumeister et al., "Does High Self-esteem Cause Better Performance," 16–17.

9. G. A. Bonanno, N. P. Field, A. Kovacevic, and S. Kaltman, "Self-enhancement as a Buffer Against Extreme Adversity: Civil War in Bosnia and Traumatic Loss in the United States," *Personality and Social Psychology Bulletin* 28 (2002): 184–96.

10. J. W. Atkinson, "Motivational Determinants of Risk Taking Behavior," *Psychological Review* 64, no. 6 (1957): 359–72.

11. R. F. Baumeister, D. M. Tice, and D. G. Hutton, "Self-Presentational Motivations and Personality Differences in Self-esteem," *Journal of Personality* 57, no. 2 (1989): 547–79.

12. R. F. Baumeister, J. C. Hamilton, and D. M. Tice, "Public Versus Private Expectancy of Success: Confidence Booster or Performance Pressure?" *Journal of Personality and Social Psychology* 48, no. 6 (1985): 1447–57.

13. Baumeister et al., "Self-Presentational Motivations," 553.

14. D. B. McFarlin and J. Blascovich, "Effects of Self-esteem and Performance Feedback on Future Affective Preferences and Cognitive Expectations," *Journal of Personality and Social Psychology* 40, no. 3 (1981): 521–31.

15. Baumeister et al., "Self-Presentational Motivations," 557.

16. S. J. Heine, D. R. Lehman, H. R. Markus, and S. Kitayama, "Is There a Universal Need for Positive Self-regard?" *Psychological Review* 106, no. 4 (1999): 766–94.

17. E. E. Jones and X. Pittman, "Toward a General Theory of Strategic Self-Presentation," in *Psychological Perspectives on the Self*, Vol. 1, ed. J. Suls (Hillsdale, NJ: Erlbaum, 1982), 231–62.

18. J. Kruger and D. Dunning, "Unskilled and Unaware of It: How Difficulties in Recognizing One's Own Incompetence Lead to Inflated Self-assessments," *Journal of Personality and Social Psychology* 77, no. 6 (1999): 1121–34.

19. M. R. Leary, "Motivational and Emotional Aspects of the Self," *Annual Review of Psychology* 58 (2007): 317–44.

20. P. Gilbert, "Evolution and Social Anxiety: The Role of Attraction, Social Competition, and Social Hierarchies," *Psychiatric Clinics of North America* 24, no. 4 (2001): 723–51.

21. F. Vertue, "From Adaptive Emotion to Dysfunction: An Attachment Perspective on Social Anxiety Disorder," *Personality and Social Psychology Review* 7, no. 2 (2003): 170–91.

22. J. Bowlby, *Attachment: Attachment and Loss*, Vol. 1, 2nd ed. (New York; Basic Books, 1982).

23. K. Bartholomew, "Avoidance of Intimacy: An Attachment Perspective," *Journal of Social and Personal Relationships* 7, no. 2 (1990): 147–78.

24. E. L. Thorndike, "Intelligence and Its Uses," *Harper's Magazine*, January 1920.

25. R. Hogan and T. Chamorro-Premuzic, "Personality and the Laws of History," in *The Wiley-Blackwell Handbook of Individual Differences*, ed. T. Chamorro-Premuzic, S. von Stumm, and A. Furnham (Oxford, UK: Wiley-Blackwell, 2011).

26. D. M. Tice, J. L. Butler, M. B. Muraven, and A. M. Stillwell, "When Modesty Prevails: Differential Favorability of Self-Presentation to Friends and Strangers," *Journal of Personality and Social Psychology* 69, no. 6 (1995): 1120–38.

27. L. Wheeler and J. Nezlek, "Sex Differences in Social Participation," *Journal of Personality and Social Psychology* 35, no. 10 (1977): 742–54.

28. B. M. DePaulo, D. A. Kashy, S. E. Kirkendol, M. M. Wyer, and J. A. Epstein,"Lying in Everyday Life," *Journal of Personality and Social Psychology* 70, no. 5 (1996): 979–95.

29. R. F. Baumeister and K. J. Cairns, "Repression and Self-Presentation: When Audiences Interfere with Self-deceptive Strategies," *Journal of Personality and Social Psychology* 62, no. 5 (1992): 851–62.

30. L. Uziel, "Rethinking Social Desirability Scales: From Impression Management to Interpersonally Oriented Self-control," *Perspectives on Psychological Science* 5, no. 3 (2010): 243–62.

31. D. B. Guralnik, ed., *Webster's New World Dictionary of the American Language* (New York: New American Library, 1984).

32. B. A. Pontari and B. R. Schlenker, "The Influence of Cognitive Load on Self-Presentation: Can Cognitive Busyness Help as Well as Harm Social Performance?" *Journal of Personality and Social Psychology* 78, no. 6 (2000): 1092–1108.

33. Ibid., 1102.

34. D. Carnegie, *How to Win Friends and Influence People* (New York: Simon & Schuster, 1936).

35. E. D. Heggestad and M. J. Morrison, "An Inductive Exploration of the Social Effectiveness Construct Space," *Journal of Personality* 76, no. 4 (2008): 839–74.

Chapter 6: A Loving Relationship

1. For a review of cultural differences in attractiveness criteria, see V. Swami and A. Furnham, eds., *Body Beautiful: Evolutionary and Socio-Cultural Perspectives* (Basingstoke, UK: Palgrave Macmillan, 2008).

2. M. T. Gabriel, J. W. Critelli, and J. S. Ee, "Narcissistic Illusions in Self-evaluations of Intelligence and Attractiveness," *Journal of Personality* 62, no. 1 (1994): 143–55.

3. The study found a correlation of just .13 between self-rated and actual attractiveness. In other words, knowing that someone is attractive would translate into a 56.5 percent probability of that person seeing himself or herself as attractive, while knowing that someone is unattractive would translate into a 56.5 percent probability of that person seeing himself or herself as unattractive.

4. Baumeister et al., "Does High Self-esteem Cause Better Performance," 1.

5. "Dating in the Dark," Wikipedia, http://en.wikipedia.org/wiki/Dating_in_the_Dark.

6. M. D. Back, L. Penke, S. C. Schmukle, K. Sachse, P. Borkenau, and J. B. Asendorpf, "Why Mate Choices Are Not as Reciprocal as We Assume: The Role of Personality, Flirting and Physical Attractiveness," *European Journal of Personality* 25, no. 2 (2011): 120–32.

7. Ibid., 125.

8. V. Coren, "The Curse of True Love," *Observer*, October 14, 2006, http://www.guardian.co.uk/commentisfree/2006/oct/15/comment.victoriacoren.

9. E. J. Finkel, P. W. Eastwick, B. R. Karney, H. T. Reis, and S. Sprecher, "Online Dating: A Critical Analysis from the Perspective of Psychological Science," *Psychological Science in the Public Interest* 13, no. 1 (2012): 1–64.

10. J. Nicholson, "Why You Shouldn't Believe in Soul Mates," *Psychology Today*, July 9, 2012, http://www.psychologytoday.com/blog/the-attraction-doctor/201207/why-you-shouldnt-believe-in-soul-mates.

11. C. E. Rusbult, M. Kumashiro, K. E. Kubacka, and E. J. Finkel, "'The Part of Me That You Bring Out': Ideal Similarity and the Michelangelo Phenomenon," *Journal of Personality and Social Psychology* 96, no. 1 (2009): 61–82.
12. J. A. Gold, R. M. Ryckman, and N. R. Mosley, "Romantic Mood Induction and Attraction to a Dissimilar Other: Is Love Blind?" *Personality and Social Psychology Bulletin* 10, no. 3 (1984): 358–68.

Chapter 7: A Healthier Life

1. M. B. Holstein and M. Minkler, "Self, Society, and the 'New Gerontology,'" *Gerontologist* 43, no. 6 (2003): 787–96.
2. W. J. Strawbridge, M. I. Wallhagen, and R. D. Cohen, "Successful Aging and Well-being: Self-Rated Compared with Rowe and Kahn," *Gerontologist* 42, no. 6 (2002): 727–33.
3. M. L. Kern and H. S. Friedman, "Personality and Differences in Health and Longevity," in *The Wiley-Blackwell Handbook of Individual Differences*, ed. T. Chamorro-Premuzic, A. Furnham, and S. von Stumm (Oxford: Wiley-Blackwell, 2011), 461–90.
4. M. F. Scheier and C. S. Carver, "Optimism, Coping, and Health: Assessment and Implications of Generalized Outcome Expectancies," *Health Psychology* 4, no. 3 (1985): 219–47.
5. P. S. Fry and D. L. Debats, "Perfectionism and the Five-Factor Personality Traits as Predictors of Mortality in Older Adults," *Journal of Health Psychology* 14, no. 4 (2009): 513–24.
6. S. C. Segerstrom, "Optimism and Immunity: Do Positive Thoughts Always Lead to Positive Effects?" *Brain, Behavior, and Immunity* 19, no. 3 (2005): 195–200.
7. Kern and Friedman, "Personality and Differences in Health and Longevity," 474.
8. A. Harvey, E. Towner, M. Peden, H. Soori, and K. Bartolomeos, "Injury Prevention and the Attainment of Child and Adolescent Health," *Bulletin of the World Health Organization* 87, no. 5 (2009): 390–94.

9. P. Fischer, T. Greitemeyer, A. Kastenmüller, C. Vogrincic, and A. Sauer, "The Effects of Risk-Glorifying Media Exposure on Risk-Positive Cognitions, Emotions, and Behaviors: A Meta-analytic Review," *Psychological Bulletin* 137, no. 3 (2011): 367–90.

10. A. Mokdad, J. Marks, D. Stroup, and J. Gerberding, "Actual Causes of Death in the United States, 2000," *Journal of the American Medical Association* 291, no. 10 (2004): 1238–45.

11. H. J. Eysenck, "Personality and Cigarette Smoking," *Life Sciences* 3, no. 7 (1964): 777–92.

12. A. R. Helgason, M. Fredrikson, T. Dyba, and G. Steineck, "Introverts Give Up Smoking More Often Than Extroverts," *Personality and Individual Differences* 18, no. 4 (1995): 559–60.

13. N. Emler, *Self-esteem: the Costs and Causes of Low Self-worth* (York, UK: Joseph Rowntree Foundation, 2001).

14. M. J. Sharp and J. G. Getz, "Substance Use as Impression Management," *Personality and Social Psychology Bulletin* 22, no. 1 (1996): 60–67.

15. N. D. Weinstein, "Unrealistic Optimism About Illness Susceptibility: Conclusions from a Community-wide Sample," *Journal of Behavioral Medicine* 10 (1987): 481–500.

16. H. S. Friedman and L. R. Martin, *The Longevity Project: Surprising Discoveries for Health and Long Life from the Landmark Eight-Decade Study* (New York: Hudson Street Press, 2011), 9.

17. C. Paul, J. Fitzjohn, P. Herbison, and N. Dickson, "The Determinants of Sexual Intercourse Before Age 16 in a Birth Cohort," *Journal of Adolescent Health* 27 (2000): 136–47.

18. G. E. Smith, M. Gerrard, and F. X. Gibbons, "Self-esteem and the Relation Between Risk Behavior and Perceived Vulnerability," *Health Psychology* 16 (1997): 137–46.

19. J. M. Burger and L. Burns, "The Illusion of Unique Invulnerability and the Use of Effective Contraception," *Personality and Social Psychology Bulletin* 14, no. 2 (1988): 264–70.

20. M. Kleinjan, R. J. van den Eijnden, and R. C. Engels, "Adolescents' Rationalizations to Continue Smoking: The Role of Disengagement

Beliefs and Nicotine Dependence in Smoking Cessation," *Addictive Behaviors* 34, no. 5 (2009): 440–45.

21. J. W. Brehm, "Postdecision Changes in the Desirability of Alternatives," *Journal of Abnormal Psychology* 52, no. 3 (1956): 384–89.

22. H. Blanton, B. W. Pelham, T. DeHart, and M. Carvallo, "Overconfidence as Dissonance Reduction," *Journal of Experimental Social Psychology* 37, no. 5 (2001): 373–85.

23. J. Jaccard, T. Dodge, and V. Guilamo-Ramos, "Metacognition, Risk Behavior, and Risk Outcomes: The Role of Perceived Intelligence and Perceived Knowledge," *Health Psychology* 24, no. 2 (2005): 161–70.

24. Blanton et al., "Overconfidence as Dissonance Reduction," 373.

25. Baumeister et al., "Does High Self-esteem Cause Better Performance," 31.

26. S. G. Tallentyre, *Voltaire in His Letters, Being a Selection from His Correspondence* (New York and London: G. P. Putnam's Sons, 1919).

27. H. Tennen and G. Affleck, "The Puzzles of Self-esteem: A Clinical Perspective," in *Self-esteem: The Puzzle of Low Self-regard*, ed. R. Baumeister (Hoboken, NJ: Wiley, 1993), 241–62.

28. Baumeister et al., "Does High Self-esteem Cause Better Performance?"

29. Y. Benyamini and O. Raz, "'I Can Tell You If I'll Really Lose All That Weight': Dispositional and Situated Optimism as Predictors of Weight Loss Following a Group Intervention," *Journal of Applied Social Psychology* 37, no. 4 (2007): 844–61.

30. M. Gerrard, F. X. Gibbons, M. Reis-Bergan, and D. W. Russell, "Self-esteem, Self-serving Cognitions, and Health Risk Behavior," *Journal of Personality* 68, no. 6 (2000): 1177–1201.

31. Gerrard et al., "Self-esteem, Self-serving Cognitions."

32. D. A. Raynor and H. Levine, "Associations Between the Five-Factor Model of Personality and Health Behaviors Among College Students," *Journal of American College Health* 58, no. 1 (2009): 73–81.

33. R. Buehler, D. Griffin, and M. Ross, "Exploring the 'Planning Fallacy': Why People Underestimate Their Task Completion

Times," *Journal of Personality and Social Psychology* 67, no. 3 (1994): 366–81.

34. T. A. Wadden, S. N. Steen, B. J. Wingate, and G. D. Foster, "Psychosocial Consequences of Weight Reduction: How Much Weight Loss Is Enough?" *American Journal of Clinical Nutrition* 63, no. 3 (1996): 461S–465S.

35. R. Goldbeck, P. Myatt, and T. Aitchison, "End-of-Treatment Self-efficacy: A Predictor of Abstinence," *Addiction* 92, no. 3 (1997): 313–24.

36. S. Allsop and B. Saunders, "Relapse and Alcohol Problems," in *Relapse and Addictive Behaviour*, ed. M. Gossop (New York: Tavistock/Routledge, 1989), 11–40.

37. J. J. Arnett, "Optimistic Bias in Adolescent and Adult Smokers and Nonsmokers," *Addictive Behaviors* 25, no. 4 (2000): 625–32.

38. S. Cohen, E. Lichtenstein, J. O. Prochaska, J. S. Rossi, E. R. Gritz, C. R. Carr, C. T. Orleans, et al., "Debunking Myths About Self-Quitting: Evidence from 10 Prospective Studies of Persons Who Attempted to Quit Smoking by Themselves," *American Psychologist* 44, no. 11 (1989): 1355–65.

39. J. O. Prochaska, W. F. Velicer, E. Guadagnoli, J. S. Rossi, and C. C. DiClemente, "Patterns of Change: Dynamic Typology Applied to Smoking Cessation," *Multivariate Behavioral Research* 26, no. 1 (1991): 83–107.

40. M. Muraven and R. F. Baumeister, "Self-regulation and Depletion of Limited Resources: Does Self-control Resemble a Muscle?" *Psychological Bulletin* 126, no. 2 (2000): 247–59.

41. J. O. Prochaska, C. C. DiClemente, and J. C. Norcross, "In Search of How People Change: Applications to Addictive Behaviors," *American Psychologist* 47, no. 9 (1992): 1102–14; J. O. Prochaska and W. F. Velicer, "The Transtheoretical Model of Health Behavior Change," *American Journal of Health Promotion* 12, no. 1 (1997): 38–48.

42. K. D. Brownell, "Personal Responsibility and Control over Our Bodies: When Expectation Exceeds Reality," *Health Psychology* 10, no. 5 (1991): 303–10.

43. K. Trottier, J. Polivy, and C. P. Herman, "Effects of Expectations About Outcomes on Self-Change Resolutions" (forthcoming).

44. J. Polivy and C. P. Herman, "The Effects of Resolving to Diet on Restrained and Unrestrained Eaters: The 'False Hope Syndrome,'" *International Journal of Eating Disorders* 26, no. 4 (1999): 434–47.

45. J. Polivy and C. P. Herman, "If at First You Don't Succeed: False Hopes of Self-Change," *American Psychologist* 57, no. 9 (2002): 677–89.

46. The original role of depression may have been to help us process negative events, but one of its malfunctions is the tendency to detach us from reality so that we can avoid further blows. In line, Freud distinguished between normal and pathological reactions to loss. In mourning (the normal reaction), we temporarily turn away from reality because it is too painful to see that our loved one is no longer there; in melancholia (Freud's version of depression), we stay detached from reality for too long, because we want to avoid future blows.

47. Polivy and Herman, "If at First You Don't Succeed," 686.

48. S. V. Zagona and L. A. Zurcher Jr., "An Analysis of Some Psychosocial Variables Associated with Smoking Behavior in a College Sample," *Psychological Reports* 17, no. 3 (1965): 967–78.

49. S. Schachter, "Recidivism and Self-Cure of Smoking and Obesity," *American Psychologist* 37, no. 4 (1982): 436–44.

50. F. Gino, A. W. Brooks, and M. E. Schweitzer, "Anxiety, Advice, and the Ability to Discern: Feeling Anxious Motivates Individuals to Seek and Use Advice," *Journal of Personality and Social Psychology* 102, no. 3 (2012): 497–512.

51. R. M. Pinkhasov, J. Wong, J. Kashanian, M. Lee, D. B. Samadi, M. M. Pinkhasov, and R. Shabsigh, "Are Men Shortchanged on Health? Perspective on Health Care Utilization and Health Risk Behavior in Men and Women in the United States," *International Journal of Clinical Practice* 64, no. 4 (2010): 475–87.

52. The authors' conclusion sums up the big picture rather clearly. Men tend to drink more often than women. Alcohol intake can cause a

range of serious chronic health conditions as well as, for example, car accidents, fires, sporting injuries, and those self-inflicted.

53. "The Biggest Loser," NBCUniversal, http://www.biggestloser.com/.
54. UK edition.
55. Approved verbatim from personal correspondence (July 2012).
56. L. Gauvin and J. C. Spence, "Physical Activity and Psychological Well-being: Knowledge Base, Current Issues, and Caveats," *Nutrition Reviews* 54, no. 4 (1996): S53–65.
57. C. B. Taylor, J. F. Sallis, and R. Needle, "The Relation of Physical Activity and Exercise to Mental Health," *Public Health Reports* 100, no. 2 (1985): 195–202.
58. Baumeister et al., "Does High Self-esteem Cause Better Performance?"

Chapter 8: Easier Said Than Done?

1. Baumeister et al., "Does High Self-esteem Cause Better Performance," 1.
2. T. B. Kashdan, V. Barrios, J. P. Forsyth, and M. F. Steger, "Experiential Avoidance as a Generalized Psychological Vulnerability: Comparisons with Coping and Emotion Regulation Strategies," *Behaviour Research and Therapy* 44, no. 9 (2006): 1301–20.
3. W. C. Thompson, G. T. Fong, and D. L. Rosenhan, "Inadmissible Evidence and Juror Verdicts," *Journal of Personality and Social Psychology* 40, no. 3 (1981): 453–63.
4. D. M. Wegner, R. Wenzlaff, R. M. Kerker, and A. E. Beattie, "Incrimination Through Innuendo: Can Media Questions Become Public Answers?" *Journal of Personality and Social Psychology* 40, no. 5 (1981): 822–32.
5. A. Tversky and D. Kahneman, "Judgment Under Uncertainty: Heuristics and Biases," *Science* 185, no. 4157 (1974): 1124–31.
6. J. Polivy and C. P. Herman, "Dieting and Binging: A Causal Analysis," *American Psychologist* 40, no. 2 (1985): 193–201.

7. I. L. Janis, "Preventing Pathogenic Denial by Means of Stress Inoculation," in *The Denial of Stress*, ed. S. Breznitz (New York: International Universities Press, 1983), 35–76.

8. J. W. Pennebaker, "Inhibition and Cognition: Toward an Understanding of Trauma and Disease," *Canadian Psychology* 26 (1985): 82–95.

9. J. J. Gross and O. P. John, "Individual Differences in Two Emotion Regulation Processes: Implications for Affect, Relationships, and Well-being," *Journal of Personality and Social Psychology* 85, no. 2 (2003): 348–62.

10. R. F. Baumeister and T. F. Heatherton, "Self-regulation Failure: An Overview," *Psychological Inquiry* 7 (1996): 1–15.

11. C. N. Macrae, G. V. Bodenhausen, A. B. Milne, and J. Jetten, "Out of Mind but Back in Sight: Stereotypes on the Rebound," *Journal of Personality and Social Psychology* 67, no. 5 (1994): 808–17.

12. Ask yourself the following question: "If I could change either my confidence or my competence, which would I pick?" People worry about their confidence because they think it affects their competence (e.g., "I have social anxiety, which stops me from speaking to people"; "I will never be able to swim because I don't feel confident enough to go in the water"), so the very reason for boosting their confidence is to boost their performance.

13. P. Arden, *Whatever You Think, Think the Opposite* (New York: Portfolio Trade, 2006), 22.

14. C. Anderson, S. Brion, D. A. Moore, and J. A. Kennedy, "A Status-Enhancement Account of Overconfidence," *Journal of Personality and Social Psychology* 103, no. 4 (2012): 718–35.

15. D. D. P. Johnson, *Overconfidence and War: The Havoc and Glory of Positive Illusions* (Cambridge, MA: Harvard University Press, 2004).

16. Data refers mostly to the year 2011. "World Economic and Financial Surveys: World Economic Outlook Database, April 2012," International Monetary Fund, http://www.imf.org/external/pubs/ft/weo/2012/01/weodata/index.aspx.

17. D. Winsborough, R. B. Kaiser, and R. Hogan, "An Evolutionary View: What Followers Want from Their Leaders," *Leadership in Action* 29, no. 3 (2009): 8–11.

18. G. Acs, *Downward Mobility from the Middle Class: Waking Up from the American Dream* (Pew Charitable Trusts, 2011), http://www .pewtrusts.org/our_work_report_detail.aspx?id=85899363697.

Index

smoking *(cont.)*
  rates of, 16
  sex differences in, 200
social confidence and people skills,
    117–49
  adaptive value of lower social
    confidence, 126–28
  assessment of, 128–29
  and childhood experiences, 132–35
  delusional overconfidence in, 118
  enhancement of, 128–32
  and fear of rejection, 127
  genetic basis of, 133, 148
  and increasing competence, 135–47
  and influencing others, 135–36,
    141–47, 149
  misjudgment of, 118–19, 147
  and motivation, 130–32
  and pessimistic realism, 128–29, 148
  and popularity, 119
  and presentational strategy, 121–24,
    138, 147–48
  and reading people, 135–37, 149
  as related to competence, 118, 120,
    127, 128, 147
  and self-focused attention,
    129–30, 148
  and self-presentation, 135–36,
    137–41, 149
  and social knowledge, 135–36
  toxicity of high social confidence,
    124–26
social media, 5–6, 50, 56
Socrates, 85, 207
Spears, Britney, 56
stoicism, 27
Stone, Dan, 48–49

Strawbridge, William, 180
Sun Tzu, 42

talent, 96–99, 108
teenagers, 8
television viewing, 8
ten-thousand-hour rule, 108
testosterone, 43
Thomson, Andy, 27
thought suppression, 208–9
Trivers, Robert, 21
Trump, Donald, 101
trustworthiness, 99–100
Tulgan, Bruce, 108
Twenge, Jean, 4, 9
Twitter, 56

upward comparison, 31

Vertue, Frances, 133
The Voice (television series), 88
Voltaire, 85, 193

weight issues and weight loss
  and *The Biggest Loser*, 202–3, 214
  and goal setting, 197
  and optimism, 193
  and personal responsibility,
    198, 203
  and thought suppression, 209
Wilde, Oscar, 167
Williams, Robbie, 55
willpower, 207–10, 213, 214, 215
work ethic, 102, 107–9, 115
Wosinska, Wilhelmina, 71–72

Zuckerberg, Mark, 97, 235n3